AT THE C

AT THE CROSS

MEDITATIONS
ON PEOPLE
WHO WERE THERE

Richard Bauckham & Trevor Hart

With Illustrations by Helen Firth

DARTON · LONGMAN + TODD

Published in Great Britain in 1999 by
Darton, Longman and Todd Ltd
1 Spencer Court
140–142 Wandsworth High Street
London SW18 4JJ

First published in the USA in 1998 by
InterVarsity Press, Downers Grove, Illinois

ISBN 0–232–52311–8

A catalogue record for this book is available from the British Library

Designed and produced by Sandie Boccacci
in QuarkXPress on an Apple PowerMac
Set in 11^1/4/14^1/3pt Bernhard Modern
Printed and bound in Great Britain by
Redwood Books, Trowbridge, Wiltshire

Acknowledgements

'In the Midst of the Company', reprinted in chapter 1, is excerpted from *All Desires Known*, by Janet Morley, copyright © Janet Morley 1988, 1992, and reproduced by permission of Morehouse Publishing, Harrisburg, Pennsylvania and by permission of SPCK, London. 'Ballad of the Judas Tree', reprinted in chapter 2, is used by permission of the author, Ruth Etchells. Excerpt from *Taken on Trust*, copyright © 1993 by Terry Waite, reprinted by permission of Harcourt, Brace & Company and by Hodder & Stoughton. 'He Went Out and Wept Bitterly', reprinted in chapter 3, is taken from Reid Isaac, *Conversations with the Crucified*, reprinted by permission of HarperCollins Publishers, New York. 'Sharing Christ's Cross in Santiago', reprinted in chapter 7, is taken from *Audacity to Believe* by Sheila Cassidy, published and copyright 1992 by Darton, Longman and Todd. The poem reprinted in 'Sharing Christ's Cross in Santiago' is taken from *Listen Pilgrim* by Christopher William Jones, published and copyright 1968 by Darton, Longman and Todd. 'God in the Darkness', reprinted in chapter 8, is taken from Nicholas Wolterstorff, *Lament for a Son*, copyright 1987 Wm. B. Eerdmans Publishing Company. Used by permission of the publisher. 'High and Lifted Up', reprinted in chapter 9, is used by permission of Hodder & Stoughton. 'The Tempter', reprinted in chapter 10, is taken from *Speaking of God* by Trevor Dennis, published in 1992 by SPCK and used by permission of the publishers. Every effort has been made to trace and contact all copyright holders for all material quoted in this book. The authors will be pleased to rectify any omissions in future editions if notified by copyright holders.

For the congregation of St Andrew's,
St Andrews

CONTENTS

PREFACE

While Jesus is the central character in the Gospel stories of his passion and death, there are also many other characters who relate in very different ways to Jesus and the events of the first Good Friday. One way in which we can enter imaginatively into these events, find ourselves in the story and respond for ourselves to the Jesus who suffered and died for us is to get to know these characters and to view the events through their eyes. Eleven such characters are the subjects of this book. We hope that, by reflecting on the ways in which Jesus and his cross touched the lives of these eleven people, readers will find that Jesus and his cross touch their own lives in new ways or with new depth.

The Gospels tell us much more about some of these eleven characters than about others, but in each case there is sufficient to bring
them to life, provided we are willing to enter imaginatively into their
situations as the Gospels sketch them for us. Narratives like the
Gospels deliberately leave much to the imagination, restricting
themselves to the essentials and thereby inviting their readers to participate in the narration. Imaginative reflection on the characters in
the Gospel stories can stimulate prayerful meditation on our own
lives.

The book is designed for more than just reading. At the beginning
of each chapter we have indicated one or more Bible passages. These
are the texts around which the chapter is written. You may wish to go
back to these texts while or after reading the chapter. The chapter
may set you on paths of reflection along which you can continue by
returning to the texts and developing your own dialogue with them.
At the end of each chapter there is a section headed "For Prayer &
Reflection." This contains a prayer or a meditation, where you may
find starting points for your own prayers. It may also contain one or
two extracts from other authors, chosen for their capacity to stimulate reflection. Integral to each chapter is a picture of the character
(from woodcuts by Helen Firth). These have been created out of
meditative consideration of each character to aid you in your own
imaginative involvement in each character's story. We hope you will
spend time with the pictures as well as pondering the texts.

The book developed out of Good Friday services that we led in
1996 and 1997 in St. Andrew's Church, St. Andrews. We are grate-
ful to the rector, Bob Gillies, who invited us to do so, to many
members of the congregation who took part in the services in various
ways and to all who encouraged us by conveying their appreciation.

Richard Bauckham
Trevor Hart

1

MARY OF BETHANY:

THE WOMAN TO BE REMEMBERED

Readings: Mark 14:3–9; John 11:55–12:7

When did Jesus' way to the cross begin? We could say that it began as far back as his baptism or more recently at his transfiguration. That was the point at which Jesus began to teach his disciples that the path God now required him to travel would lead to suffering, rejection and death, though the disciples did not understand and did not want to know. We could say that Jesus' way to the cross began when he set out on his last journey to Jerusalem. But the point at which it must have become clear to all who knew him that Jesus was set on walking straight into mortal danger was when he arrived in Bethany six days before the feast of the Passover.

Bethany, just over the hill from Jerusalem, was where Jesus had often stayed with his friends Lazarus, Martha and Mary. The last time he had been there, a few weeks before, he had come at Martha's and Mary's request and had brought their brother Lazarus back to life. He had kept away from Jerusalem, because by then the determination of the Jewish authorities in the city to arrest him was clear. When Jesus raised Lazarus from death, Jerusalem was already a dangerous place for him to be. After he raised Lazarus, it became even more dangerous. The miracle was famous. The chief priests were afraid of the political consequences of his reputation with the people. They planned his execution should he return to Jerusalem, as he might well be expected to do for the most important festival of the Jewish year, the Passover. And when the crowds of pilgrims began to pour into the city and its neighborhood a week before the festival, the authorities made it generally known that Jesus was a wanted man. Anyone who set eyes on him should report it to the authorities.

When Jesus arrives with his disciples in Bethany, one of the first things his friends there surely tell him is the extreme danger he is in. When they take Jesus into their home, they are not just giving him hospitality; they are hiding a wanted man. No doubt they try to keep his visit secret. No doubt they realize they are putting themselves in danger by harboring a man they should be reporting to the authorities. No doubt the disciples who have traveled with Jesus are acutely aware of the danger they are putting themselves in too. So when the Bethany family lay on a celebratory meal to welcome Jesus the evening he arrives, the atmosphere is tense with danger. Perhaps for some of the disciples the danger is exciting. They are not expecting Jesus to be arrested. Instead they expect him to summon the armies of heaven and take over Jerusalem by supernatural force. For others, who know Jesus better, there is fear and foreboding. The great cause to which they have devoted their lives in recent months is going to end in tragedy. The man they have devoted their lives to is risking it all by walking foolishly, heedlessly, incomprehensibly but unstoppably into a deathtrap.

The meal is a very special one for the sisters Martha and Mary. They owe their brother's life to Jesus. They want to express their gratitude. It is an occasion for joy: the joy of having Lazarus back with them, the joy of having Jesus, who restored Lazarus to them, also back with them. But every feeling of joy and every expression of pleasure is overlaid by their awareness that it may well be the very last time that Jesus is with them. When he walks over the Mount of Olives into Jerusalem the next morning, as he clearly intends to do, the chances are that he will be arrested.

Martha, the more practical, the more responsible, probably the older of the two sisters, shows her love and gratitude to Jesus in a fairly conventional way. She serves the meal. Even though she probably has servants, she serves the meal herself. It is a way of showing her gratitude that is no doubt approved and appreciated. It raises no eyebrows. But Mary, the less conventional sister, who has always taken being a disciple of Jesus to unconventional lengths, now does something that has most of the people around the table indignant with disapproval.

To understand what Mary does we need to understand the conventions of hospitality and courtesy to a guest. One thing any host would do when guests arrived for dinner was to see that they got their feet washed. After a day of walking in open sandals on Middle Eastern roads, feet were hot, dirty and smelly and needed washing. It was a menial, rather unpleasant task that servants would do. If no servants were available, the host would provide water and towels for the guests to wash their own feet. No one would expect a host to do it personally for a guest. Another thing a host might do for an honored guest was to anoint his head with sweet-smelling oil, the sort of oil people used the way we use soap.

What does Mary do? She performs both these services for Jesus but with a kind of exaggeration and extravagance that astonishes the guests. To anoint Jesus' head she uses a vastly expensive flask of perfume. It was one of those perfumes that were enormously valued in the ancient world and cost a fortune because they came from so far away. This one came from the Himalayas. A family could have lived for a year on the price of this perfume. The flask itself was precious, made of alabaster and so constructed to keep the perfume in that the neck of the flask had to be broken to release the perfume. But not content to pour it on Jesus' head, Mary uses it to wash his feet. Instead of letting a servant wash Jesus' feet, she does it herself. And instead of offering him water and a towel for the purpose, she uses the spikenard and wipes Jesus' feet with her own hair.

Mary says nothing. In that respect she stays within the social conventions. For a woman to break into the men's conversation on an occasion like this was not done. But what she does speaks far louder than any words she could have found. Mary is the last person to be constrained by the social conventions. What she does is the conventional thing in a thoroughly unconventional way. The extravagance of her love for Jesus is expressed in the unconventional extravagance of her act. What she has to express requires her to do something expressive enough for the purpose. And Jesus sees this. He values and praises what she has done. Wherever the Gospel is preached in all the world, he says, Mary's deed will be far more memorable than anything she could have said.

What is it then that Mary expresses? Her love and gratitude to Jesus? Yes, but more than that. Mary knows as well as anyone there, perhaps better than anyone, that Jesus faces imminent death. Mary shares the mixture of joy and foreboding, the bittersweet atmosphere of this occasion. She expresses her devotion to Jesus so extravagantly because it may well be the last opportunity she will ever have to do so. It is the last act she can do for him. It is as though she were anointing his body for the burial she realizes is soon to happen. She pours her love for Jesus into this last act for him, just as the bereaved would go to expense and trouble over the burial of a loved one because it is the last and now the only way they can express their love for him. So Jesus says, 'She has performed a good service for me . . . She has done what she could; she has anointed my body beforehand for its burial.'

What is most important to grasp about Mary's act is that in this way she shows she accepts that Jesus is to die. Perhaps alone among the disciples gathered at this meal, Mary accepts that Jesus is to die. She doesn't think of trying to dissuade him from going to Jerusalem. She doesn't think that God is going to save him from death, as probably some of the disciples did. She doesn't think of trying to save him from death, as Peter is going to do later. She doesn't suppose that Jesus' death can be avoided. She anticipates and accepts that Jesus is to die. This is why her act of extravagant love amounts to anointing his body for burial. It is not, of course, that she loves Jesus any less than other disciples do. Nor does she understand why Jesus is walking open-eyed into virtually certain death. No more than any of the disciples does Mary understand why Jesus' death should be God's will for him. It is simply that Mary sees that Jesus himself fully accepts his coming death as the destiny he has to fulfill. She does not understand but nor does she question or resist this path that Jesus is taking. Her love for him enables her to intuit his conviction of God's will and to accept it as he does. Because it is what he knows he must do she also accepts it.

This is Mary's importance. This is why she is to be remembered.

This is why Jesus makes this remarkable statement about her, comparable with nothing he says about anyone else: 'Truly I tell you, wherever the good news is proclaimed in the whole world, what she has done will be told in remembrance of her.' What she has done is to be told as part of the gospel story, because it goes to the heart of the gospel. It anticipates the cross of Jesus. Alone among the disciples, Mary recognizes that the cross is Jesus' necessary, God-given destiny.

So it is with Mary's insight that we too must approach the cross. Like Mary, we may not understand its necessity. We may understand more later. But we need to begin with accepting, as Mary does, Jesus' own acceptance of the cross as the way he must go, accepting his cross as the Father's will for him, as God's will for us, as the way that Jesus had to go for us and for our salvation. In human terms Jesus should not have died. His death was not just or right; it was judicial murder. We know that too. But nevertheless Jesus accepted the injustice of his death as the way his obedience to his Father must lead him. That must be our starting point in approaching the cross, provided we accept it, as Mary did, in loving devotion to Jesus, seeking ourselves to enter into that mysterious necessity of obedience to death which Jesus accepted for us.

We have noticed the mixed emotions that surround Jesus at this meal: the joy that Jesus' friends in Bethany feel in having him with them interwoven with the sense of danger and foreboding. Mary's act corresponds to this atmosphere. At the same time it expresses her joy in Jesus' presence and presages Jesus' death. Both these things Mary's use of the perfume expresses. For people at that time, sweet-smelling oils and unguents were valued for two purposes. At a celebration, the fragrance would express the joy of the occasion and help to lift people's spirits. The Old Testament calls it 'the oil of gladness.' But perfumed oils of this kind were also used to anoint and to embalm the dead. Then the fragrance served to cover the stench of death and helped to soften the pain of the bereaved. When Mary pours out her flask of priceless oil on Jesus, John's narrative reminds us that we need, in our imagining of the scene, to bring our sense of smell into imaginative play. 'The whole house,' he says, 'was filled with the fragrance of the perfume.' Mary's act changes the atmosphere – literally and metaphorically. In accepting Jesus' death in this way, with all her devotion to Jesus poured extravagantly into her acceptance of his death, Mary's love dispels the sense of danger and foreboding. She cannot, of course, make his coming death any less terrible. The stench of death is the unavoidable reality of death. But the fragrance of love transforms it. Because Mary intuits the great love with which Jesus willingly undertakes death, her own love, responding to his, embraces the pain. The joy and its contradiction, the presentiment of loss, remain. But Mary's love for Jesus embraces both. The fragrance fills the whole house.

However, all that some of those present can think of is the waste. They cannot see the positive value in Mary's extravagance: her desire to enact her extravagant devotion to Jesus on this the last occasion that she can. Instead they see her extravagance in conventionally negative terms: 'Why was the ointment wasted in this way? For this ointment could have been sold for more than three hundred denarii, and the money given to the poor.' It is not difficult to sympathize with this reaction. One of the admirable features of Jewish piety in Jesus' time was the well-practiced duty to provide for the poor. Jesus himself had told the rich young man, who claimed to have kept all the commandments, that he lacked just one thing: he should sell all he owned and give the money to the poor. But now, at the meal in Bethany, Jesus refuses to hear this complaint about Mary's act: 'Let her alone ... She has performed a good service for me. For you always have the poor with you, and you can show kindness to them whenever you wish; but you will not always have me.'

Jesus, of course, sees that the objection is just a way of rubbishing Mary's action, and that the objectors just have not seen the point of it. The point is: 'You *always* have the poor ... You will not *always* have me.' Mary accepts that Jesus is going to die, and she responds to that situation. The people who complain want her to behave the way she could at any other time. Not having truly accepted Jesus' death themselves, they cannot see what impels her to do for Jesus what she can while she still can.

The situation Mary, but not the others, recognizes is an exceptional one. Jesus is nearing the end of his earthly life. That situation does not recur, as Jesus himself says: 'you will not always have me.' For us there cannot be an alternative. We cannot give to Jesus what we could otherwise have given to the poor, not only because Jesus is not in that sense here to have money spent on him but for a more profound reason also. The way of the cross, which Mary accepts, is the way that leads Jesus himself into his deepest solidarity with the poor. Stripped of what few possessions he had, treated with contempt and revulsion, excluded from society, left to die, Jesus in his death enters the situation of the most wretched of the earth. He identifies himself with all of us but especially with the most wretched, the suffering, the needy, the poor.

To follow the way of the cross is to enter a deeper solidarity with the poor than merely giving money to them need be. To follow Jesus on the way of the cross is to enter Jesus' solidarity with the poorest of people. To accept his death, as Mary did, is to accept that solidarity with the poor. To love Jesus now, with Mary's extravagant devotion, is to love also the poor with whom he has especially identified himself. We do not have to decide whether to give what we have to Jesus or to give it to people in need, for Jesus himself says of feeding the hungry, clothing the naked, visiting the sick and the prisoners: 'just as you did it to one of the least of these my brothers and sisters, you did it to me' (Mt 25:40 author's translation).

We should most certainly love Jesus with Mary's extravagant devotion, returning the boundless love of God for us that we encounter in Jesus' death for us. In loving Jesus and in accepting Jesus' death, we shall find ourselves drawn ever deeper into God's own loving identification with the poor and the needy and the suffering. The poor are always with us, Jesus also is with us, and it is as the brother of the poor that Jesus is with us.

For Prayer & Reflection

Lord Jesus
we remember Mary of Bethany
who understood as no one else did
the self-giving love
that took you to the cross.

With her we see
your wholehearted obedience to your Father's will
your wholehearted love for us all
that committed you to die.

With her we accept
your death
as your gift of yourself,
as God's gift of God's self
to the world.

With her we wish
to give ourselves
in devotion to you
and to the way of your cross.

Give us
the uncalculating and extravagant devotion
that will fill our lives
and those of others
with the fragrance of your love.

Open our hearts to the poor
who are always with us
and in whom you are always with us.

In the Midst of the Company
Jesus and the Woman Who Anointed His Head

In the midst of the company I sat alone,
and the hand of death took hold of me;
I was cold with secrecy,
and my God was far away.

For this fear did my mother conceive me,
and to seek this pain did I come forth?
Did her womb nourish me for the dust,
or her breasts, for me to drink bitterness?

O that my beloved would hold me
and gather me in her arms;
that the darkness of God might comfort me,
that this cup might pass me by.

I was desolate, and she came to me;
when there was neither hope nor help for pain
she was at my side;
in the shadow of the grave she has restored me.

My cup was spilling with betrayal,
but she has filled it with wine;
my face was wet with fear,
but she has anointed me with oil,
and my hair is damp with myrrh.
The scent of her love surrounds me;
it is more than I can bear.

She has touched me with authority;
in her hands I find strength.
For she acts on behalf of the broken,
and her silence is the voice of the unheard.
Though many murmur against her, I will praise her;
and in the name of the unremembered,
I will remember her.

Janet Morley

2

JUDAS ISCARIOT:
THE BETRAYER

Readings: Matthew 26:14–16, 47–50; 27:1–5

Helmut Thielicke tells the story of a man who, living amid the darkness of Hitler's Third Reich, took his stand against the National Socialist government and all that it stood for and was duly arrested. He was sent to prison where he was kept for a long time in solitary confinement, enduring regular beatings and torture as his captors sought to extract a confession that might enable them to convict him of some crime. After several months he was released without charge. Tired, physically weak and undernourished, he was nonetheless an unbroken spirit, as ardent in his opposition to the totalitarian state as he had ever been. Two weeks after his release he was found hanged, having committed suicide in his attic. Those who had followed his case with interest wondered how it was that his strength and courage had eventually been destroyed. Those who knew him well were aware of the reason. He had made the awful discovery that it was his son who had informed against him and delivered him into the hands of the Nazis. The treachery of one whom he loved finally accomplished what institutional brutality had failed to do.

Betrayal, which of its very essence involves the pain of being delivered into danger or discomfort by one loved or trusted, entails a pain that surpasses the physical kind, no matter how intense. The inner sanctum of the heart is breached, and there is no ready defense. Pain inflicted by enemies is one thing. Pain inflicted by a friend or loved one is something quite different.

Perhaps it is not surprising, therefore, that the New Testament paints a dark picture of the one who is remembered above all for having betrayed Jesus to the authorities and thereby facilitated his arrest, trial and execution. From beginning to end the account given of him by the Gospel writers is unashamedly jaundiced, as the story of his time with Jesus and the others is colored by the knowledge of his ultimate betrayal. The stigma of treachery, it seems, cannot be overlooked and forgotten by those telling the tale. Even Jesus is recorded as having had some strong things to say about the one who would betray him: he is a devil; the son of perdition; the one for whom it would have been better if he had never been born. And Judas's story ends in the awfulness of disgrace and shame, and the desperation of suicide: unable to live with the consequences of his own actions; hounded by guilt and despair into a sordid and lonely death.

How should we consider this character? What should we feel about and for him? Disgust? Anger? Bitterness? Or are we warranted in feeling sorry for him, seeing him as the victim of circumstance, as one exploited by other, more sinister forces and as undeserving of his recorded fate? And what of God? Can there be a place in the heart of God for the one who handed his only Son over to be crucified? Tradition has not for the most part supposed it to be so. Dante imaginatively invents for Judas's eternal destiny the lowest of all hells, a hell not of fire and brimstone but of cold and ice, designed for those swept not into sins of passion but into the cold, calculating sin of deliberate rejection of God's love. Can we concur with this assessment of Judas's situation?

These are powerful questions, and any answers we give to them can only be by way of exploratory and tentative musings. But it seems proper and necessary that we should address them.

Judas's sin was certainly an awful one. Here the Gospel writers are characteristically blunt in their assessment. Judas is, in the words of Luke, 'the one who became a traitor.' He is one of those figures in history who will always be remembered for one tragic incident in his life. His treachery has come to define who he was. We don't know much else about him. We don't know, for example, whether he had a difficult childhood, whether he did well at school, whether his parents had a pet name for him, or any of the myriad things that make up the complexity of a single human life. All that has been passed on for us to know is tied to his role in the story of Holy Week: how on that fateful night Judas went out from the Last Supper and led the temple guard to Jesus.

In doing so he fashioned for himself the description that would be recounted and reinforced time and time again in the telling of the story of Jesus' passion – Judas Iscariot, the one who betrayed his master and his friends. Having created the role, he found that he could not live with it. He could not face the pain of being identified for the rest of his life (no matter how often and how hard he tried to escape or make amends for it) with an action that he wanted to erase from his memory and his history. And he could see no way beyond the irreversibility of his treachery and the death and darkness to which it had seemingly led.

There is a certain injustice in the way we allow this one action to color our perception of Judas. We should remember that there was more to him than he came to at this despicable moment. None of us is simply identical with his or her darkest actions, no matter how 'natural' they may seem to feel. Nonetheless, no matter how tragic, Judas's action was an evil one. Who knows what he thought the consequences of his collaboration with the Jewish authorities would be? His terrible remorse suggests that he did not expect the trial and execution that followed. Maybe he had not allowed himself to face the question, repressing all but the most tolerable of imagined alternatives in a bid to salve his conscience and peace of mind. But we should not too quickly ascribe either worthy motives or credulousness to Judas in an effort to mitigate what was by any standards a cheap action. Deliberately handing Jesus and his friends over to those who were known enemies of the cause and who could only intend harm was at best to act with wanton disregard for their well-being and at worst consciously to put them in danger. Whichever way we choose to look at it, Judas cannot be let off the hook. His deed was a dark one.

Paradoxically, according to the same Christian tradition that has vilified him, Judas's deed was also a *necessary* one. Someone had to hand Jesus over. There had to be a traitor, a collaborator. The structure of the gospel plot demands it. 'The Son of Man,' says Jesus on the road to Jerusalem, 'will be handed over to be crucified.' It is easy to skip over the words that precede the mention of death itself, for Christian reflection on salvation has generally focused on Jesus' death as such. But that focus is helpful only if the wider background is also kept in sight. Jesus speaks not only of death but of *being given up* to death. This giving up, or handing over, is a vital part of the context that gives the death itself a particular significance and quality.

From the climax of the passion story it is clear that the pain of the cross for Jesus is never merely physical but also spiritual and relational. It has to do with his willingness to plumb the depths of the human experience of godforsakenness. In the dark hour of Golgotha the human Son of God feels separated from his Father, a pain the intensity of which we must suppose to be in direct proportion to the closeness of the relationship between them. The so-called cry of dereliction from the cross ('God, why have you abandoned me?') penetrates to the heart of what Jesus bears on Good Friday. The terrible paradox is that at the very moment when in reality he is closest to God and acting most explicitly in accordance with his Father's will, he feels delivered up, handed over and abandoned, and yet he submits himself to the intense pain of that deliverance for our sakes.

It is not death as such or even death in this horrific and debasing version but death within the context of having been 'given up' that Jesus refers to as the Messiah's lot. The dimension of that which takes place between the Son and his heavenly Father has its perverse parallel on the human plane in Judas's action. And the pain of the cross derives from this too. The suffering Messiah, who is also Immanuel, God in our midst as a human person, knows the intense hurt of the betrayal that threatens to break the spirit in ways that physical torture may not succeed in doing. In a sense, we might say that God has been being consistently betrayed ever since he created men and women capable of love and friendship and therefore betrayal. But here God fathoms a new depth of experience, learning from the human side what it is for one person to be betrayed by another, feeling the pain and anguish that treachery generates. God hands himself over to be put to death in and through the unwitting but willful cooperation of Judas's sin.

'He came to what was his own,' says John in his Gospel, 'and his own people did not accept him.' On the contrary his own actively rejected him and handed him over to the Romans to be crucified. At this point in the story of God's dealings with his people, Judas stands as representative of all those who concurred with this deliverance to death, from the religious leaders who conspired against him to the fickle crowd whose cries changed overnight from 'hosanna' to 'crucify him.' Judas's action was all part of the deal, part of the package which Jesus saw coming. So when Judas comes to the garden of Gethsemane, Jesus is not taken by surprise or thrown into a panic. He has been waiting for this and walks out to meet Judas, John tells us, 'knowing all that was about to happen to him.' And Judas hands Jesus over only because Jesus himself is willing to be handed over. Indeed, there is an important sense in which Jesus hands himself over. After all, he predicted Judas's betrayal, and it would have been easy for him to have identified the traitor and had him constrained by the other disciples. But he lets him go out into the night to do his evil deed. It is almost as if Judas's role is cosmetic. There has to be a traitor for the story to take shape, but it need not have been Judas. He merely represents the whole of humankind in its innate propensity to reject the Son of God when he draws near and to hand him over to be crucified.

It is no coincidence that the Gospels use the same word to describe Judas's sin as the New Testament uses elsewhere to describe God's action in delivering his Son up to death and the Son's own handing of himself over to death for our sakes — *paradidomi*, 'to hand over, to deliver up, to betray.' Viewed from a human angle Judas's action is a crass betrayal of one who loved him. Viewed in the wider theological context, his action is not excused of its moral orientation but is subsumed under that which had to take place, and that which God intended *should* take place in order that the sins of his people might be forgiven.

Judas, who (as Luke reminds us in Acts 1) was one of the Twelve, had been called by Jesus to a ministry of service to the gospel: of delivering or handing over (the same word is used) the message of Jesus's death and resurrection and the attendant forgiveness of sins. We might suppose that he abandoned this ministry when he betrayed the cause of the gospel by his treachery to Jesus. Or we might see that even in the darkness of this action he helped to fulfill the cause. In his tragic moment of self-condemnation, Judas served that purpose of God by which all condemnation is set aside for those who are in

Christ Jesus. It is as if Judas's treachery was the one thing that God could rely on. And Judas did not fail him.

Lastly, although Judas is consistently portrayed in the Gospels with the stigma of treachery already attached to him and although John's Gospel states that he was not to be trusted with the apostolic purse (Is this anything more than a refusal to see anything but the worst in someone who has come subsequently to a tragic misdemeanor? 'I always thought he was a bit shifty!'), little in Judas's earlier story makes him the most obvious candidate for this dark act. The disciples seem not to have jumped to any conclusions on the matter. The accounts of the Last Supper make it clear that Jesus' prediction of betrayal threw them into turmoil, each of them in turn being driven to ask, 'Lord, is it I?' In the event it was Judas, but prior to its happening it was not obvious that it would be so.

Although Judas betrayed Jesus, he was not the only one to abandon Jesus or to let him down in the events of that night. He was the first and perhaps we think the worst. But we should not forget that all the disciples fled in fear from the scene of Jesus' arrest. Even Peter, the one who had sworn openly that he would die before leaving Jesus' side, found his resolve crumbling in the face of circumstances and denied his master three times. There is more than a passing similarity between Peter's denial and subsequent remorse and Judas's betrayal and remorse. But Judas went out and did what perhaps Peter was tempted to do. He took his own life. For that reason he was not there to see the risen Christ or to discover that his sin, despicable as it was, had been used by God to further his saving purposes. What, we might wonder, would Jesus' words to Judas have been on the beach had he been there?

The least we can say is that the forgiveness offered freely to Peter and to all who will receive it must also be available for Judas. His sin was indeed awful but not so awful as to place him beyond the scope of God's love. More than that perhaps we cannot say. But that much we must. For if there is no hope for Judas, then there is little hope for

any of us. All of us in our own small way but no less significantly have
betrayed Jesus many times, and usually for a good deal less than thirty
pieces of silver.

Ruth Etchells' 'Ballad of the Judas Tree' will carry our reflections
on this theme further. The words are an imaginative construal of the
relationship between Judas and Jesus in death, which ironically
brought Judas much closer to his master than any of the other disciples, as they hung on their respective trees.

For Prayer & Reflection

Ballad of the Judas Tree

In Hell there grew a Judas Tree
Where Judas hanged and died
Because he could not bear to see
His master crucified

Our Lord descended into Hell
And found his Judas there
For ever hanging on the tree
Grown from his own despair

So Jesus cut his Judas down
And took him in his arms
'It was for this I came' he said
'And not to do you harm

My Father gave me twelve good men
And all of them I kept
Though one betrayed and one denied
Some fled and others slept

In three days' time I must return
To make the others glad
But first I had to come to Hell
And share the death you had

My tree will grow in place of yours
Its roots lie here as well
There is no final victory
Without this soul from Hell'

So when we all condemn him
As of every traitor worst
Remember that of all his men
Our Lord forgave him first

Ruth Etchells

Beirut, January 20, 1987

When I awoke, it was dusk. For a moment I lay still, slowly, reluc-
tantly returning to the conscious world. It was unusually quiet. A
gentle breeze stirred the faded hotel curtains, bringing with it a hint
of the sea. Somewhere in the building a tap was turned on, sending
the pipes in my bathroom into spasm. I swung my legs over the edge
of the bed and walked to the window. On the pavement below, the
street vendors had gone for the day. The only people left were the
journalists. They sat on the seawall, smoking, chatting, waiting like
pilgrims for a miracle. I closed the window and drew the curtains,
shutting out the last of the dying light. I had already packed to depart
for London, and now I checked my pockets: one blank memo pad,
one ballpoint pen. Nothing more. I debated with myself whether to
wear my wedding ring or lock it in my briefcase. I decided to wear it

and my watch. I tuned my small radio in to the World Service of the BBC. World News would be broadcast on the hour; it was a link with home. While I balanced the radio on my briefcase and waited for the familiar strains of 'Lillibullero' there was a knock at the door. I opened it just enough to see who was there. As I had expected, it was one of my Druze bodyguards.

'Are you ready, sir?'

I invited him in, switched off the radio and made a final check. Everything was packed. It would be a matter of minutes to collect my bags and leave for the airport. I picked up a black leather jacket from the back of a chair. My bodyguards had spent several days searching Beirut before they found one large enough to fit me. Again I checked my pockets – nothing but a pen and a notepad. My guard pointed to a bullet-proof vest lying on the bed.

'Aren't you going to wear that?'

I shook my head. If one of the kidnappers wanted to kill me, he would be near enough to shoot me in the head; a bullet-proof vest would be useless. I took a last look around the room and moved towards the door. Several more guards were standing in the corridor, each with an automatic weapon. We walked towards the lift. A guard with a chest like a beer barrel propped open the door.

'We leave by the basement.'

The antiquated lift descended slowly through the faded glory of the Riviera Hotel. With a gentle groan it touched down, and the gates were cranked open. Two men went before me, two behind. We threaded our way through the subterranean maze, emerging in a side street. I turned up my collar and hunched down into my jacket. The road was full of potholes and strewn with bricks and slabs of broken concrete. It was raining when we reached the car. I squeezed into the back, totally surrounded by protective Druze. As we drove away from the hotel, I saw the journalists still watching and waiting and hoping. In a few minutes we were in a street close to the American University of Beirut (AUB). The car stopped, and I shook hands with the guards.

'Thanks for your help. Whatever happens, don't try to follow me.'

They smiled, large, friendly, roguish smiles. 'Be careful.'

I slipped out of the car and watched them drive away. It was dark, and apart from a few parked cars, the street was deserted. In the distance I could hear the sound of shellfire as Beirut warmed up to yet another night of carnage. By now a steady rain was falling. I walked briskly up the street, looking neither left nor right, past the petrol station, past the apartments, straight to my rendezvous. As agreed, the main door was left ajar. I pushed it open and went in. In the shadows, a pair of eyes peered at me from behind the barely open door of the porter's room. I looked straight back at them, and slowly, as if by remote control, the door closed. I stepped inside the lift and ascended to the apartment of my intermediary, Dr Mroueh. He occupied two apartments in the block. One he used as his consulting rooms, the other as his residence. He opened the door as soon as I rang the bell and invited me into his study.

'Hello, Terry, good to see you again.'

He smiled nervously and lit his pipe while I looked around. Nothing had changed. The same chromium-and-glass desk, leather chairs, framed certificates on the walls. He gestured to me to sit. We chatted inconsequentially until the telephone rang. He spoke softly in Arabic for a few moments and then stood.

'I am so sorry, but I have to leave.'

'Why?'

'A patient is in labor. I am needed urgently.'

'Can't you wait a little longer?'

'That is not possible – I am sorry.'

Somewhere in the back of my head a bell, which had been ringing gently for days, increased in volume.

'I have to go to the hospital. I'll leave the door on the latch. When you leave, please lock it behind you.'

We shook hands, and he left. I crossed to the window and stared down at the empty street. It was not too late to walk away. Within a

few minutes I could be back at the hotel. I turned and looked at the
bookcase. Nothing but medical tomes. I walked down the corridor to
the surgery, slipped off my shoes and stood on the scales: 236 pounds –
almost seventeen stone. Too heavy; I ought to be fifteen stone,
probably less. I returned to the other room and paced up and down,
trying to quell my mounting anxiety. I thought of Terry Anderson
and Tom Sutherland and for a moment wondered what it was like to
be imprisoned for month after month. I had been alone in this room
for less than an hour, and already I felt the walls and ceiling pressing
in on me. I sat in one of the leather chairs and tried to regain my
composure. Then I heard it: the gentle hum of an electric motor.
Someone coming up in the lift. I stood and crossed the room. There
was a faint thud as the lift came to an abrupt halt. I heard the lift door
open, and a second later the doorbell rang. A small stocky man wear-
ing a single-breasted suit stood on the landing. He was my principal
contact with the kidnappers, and we had met previously. I could feel
his nervousness.

'Are you alone?'

'Yes.'

He stepped into the apartment. 'Are you armed?'

'No.'

'Please, I shall have to search you.' He patted my body and turned
towards the door. 'We must leave right now.'

We got into the lift and silently descended. In the lobby the
porter's door was firmly closed. We walked into the empty street and
found it was still raining. After a few paces, the man halted beside a
large car.

'You sit in the back. If we are stopped, you must say I am responsible for driving you around Beirut.'

I climbed into the back seat, and we drove out into the night. As
we went through the battered streets I remembered a similar journey
I had made years ago in Tehran. Then, as now, there were no reliable
guarantees. I got into a car totally at the mercy of kidnappers and was

driven to a secret location. The Iranian Revolutionary Guards had kept their word; they took me to the hostages they were holding and returned me to Tehran a few hours later. Now, I had been given a promise that I would be allowed to see Terry Anderson and Tom Sutherland, who, according to their captors, were depressed and ill. The kidnappers knew it was an invitation I could not refuse. It was because my contact gave me his word 'as a Muslim' that I had decided to trust him. I peered through the side windows of the car. Every minute or two a brilliant flash of light illuminated the surrealistic landscape. Only an El Greco could have captured the stark drama of the scene. The pain, the horror, the light, the shadows, the beauty, and behind it all a people suffering, weeping, dying. Suddenly, without warning, the driver pulled the car to the side of the road.

'Why do we stop here?'

'You must get out – we have a puncture.'

I knew he was lying. It was obvious that we would change cars at some point. Why tell such a stupid and pointless lie? There was another car in front of us now, with two men in police uniforms sitting inside.

'Get into the back quickly.'

The man in the suit sat beside me. 'Now, I am sorry, I must blindfold you.'

He produced a strip of curtain material and covered my eyes. It wasn't the change of car that worried me or the blindfold. I had expected both. It was the lie. From that point on I began to prepare myself for capture. We drove for half an hour or so. My companions exchanged words in Arabic. I said nothing. It was as though I had walked onto a track and all I could do now was to follow it wherever it led.

Terry Waite

Prayer

'Surely, Lord, it is not I?'

So often we know even before we ask that it is.

We,
like Judas,
like all the disciples,
like every disciple who has ever lived,
have betrayed Jesus
for the most trifling of rewards.

May we, too, feel the burn of Jesus' eyes as he speaks to us
'Yes, it is you.'

Help us Lord
to confront our secret betrayals,
to know them as clearly and judge them as surely
as does your purifying and cauterizing gaze.

And on the far side of the shame and pain of crucifixion
may we discover your enduring and redeeming love
restoring us and raising us up
to a new fullness of life lived in your Son and the power of the Holy
Spirit.

Amen.

3

PETER:

THE FAILURE

Readings: Luke 22:54–62; John 13:33–38; 18:1–11

Of the twelve disciples, Peter is the one who follows Jesus furthest on Jesus' way to the cross. With the rest of the Twelve he is at the Last Supper. He goes with Jesus to the garden of Gethsemane, and he sleeps, like the others, while Jesus wrestles in prayer with the destiny that now faces him. When the temple police arrive with Judas to arrest Jesus, Peter draws his sword to put up a fight, until Jesus stops him. With the other disciples Peter flees as Jesus is taken under guard to the high priest's house for interrogation, but unlike the others Peter follows. He follows cautiously, keeping his distance, and lurks in the courtyard of the house, waiting to hear news of what happens to Jesus.

But there Peter's following of the way of the cross ends. He gets a last glimpse of Jesus before his death, as Jesus is led away to a further interrogation, but it comes at the point when the realization that Peter has failed Jesus, denied being a disciple of Jesus, renounced Jesus, as it were, overcomes him. Peter has followed Jesus further than have the rest of the Twelve, but then he falters and fails and abandons the way of the cross long before Jesus is condemned and led away to his death. No more than any others of the Twelve is Peter there at the cross when Jesus is crucified. So, in tracing Jesus' way to the cross through the eyes of Peter, we shall be looking through the eyes of a disciple who at the crucial point abjectly fails to be a disciple. But Peter's failure will prove not at all a bad standpoint from which to see Jesus afresh.

In Mary of Bethany's act we saw her extravagant devotion to Jesus and her acceptance that Jesus must die. Peter was no less extravagantly devoted to Jesus. He protested his willingness to die for Jesus, and he certainly really meant it. But unlike Mary, Peter could not accept that Jesus must die. He wanted to die for Jesus, but he could not accept that Jesus must die for him. And because he could not accept that Jesus must die, Peter got discipleship all wrong. He was bound to fail. He had to learn through failure what being a disciple of Jesus was really all about. He had to learn through failure what Jesus himself was all about. Peter, it seems, was the sort of person who had to get things tragically wrong before he could get them right. He had to make a mess of doing things his own way before he could accept God's way. But since the cross is the place where God's love embraces failure and tragedy, there was no better place to fail than on the way to the cross. Peter's failure was precisely God's opportunity.

Of all Jesus' disciples, it is Peter we get to know best in the Gospels. After all, Peter is so often the first to speak, the first to act, the one who naturally takes the lead and steals the limelight in the stories. When Jesus wants to know what the disciples think, it is Peter who speaks for them. Peter is eager, impulsive, impetuous, bursting with self-confidence, always knowing best, always jumping straight in where angels hesitate to approach. But Peter has fine qualities. He is a natural leader. He has immense enthusiasm, courage and drive. And he is genuinely devoted to Jesus, and he genuinely wants with all his heart to be Jesus' disciple. Jesus himself marks Peter out for the leading role among his twelve apostles.

The trouble is: Peter wants Jesus to be successful. Jesus is the Messiah. Jesus is going to achieve the redemption of Israel, and Peter is going to make sure he does. So when Jesus tries to make the disciples see that the way to redemption lies through his suffering, rejection and death, Peter would not hear of it. Jesus' death would be failure, and Peter wants Jesus to be successful. By the time Peter is sitting with Jesus at table in the upper room, sharing the meal that Jesus makes into a kind of farewell celebration, of course it is obvious that Jesus is in serious danger. The talk is all of partings, betrayal, and imminent catastrophe. But Peter rises to the situation. If necessary he is prepared to lay down his life for Jesus. He will risk his own life to save Jesus from death. Maybe some of the disciples around the table are already wishing they could slip away unnoticed and run away back to Galilee. But it never crosses Peter's mind to think this. Jesus needs him. All the others might desert Jesus, but Peter never. Peter is ready for anything. This may be the crucial moment at which Peter must ensure Jesus' success. If he has to lay down his life for Jesus, it will be a heroic death for a heroic cause.

Is Peter being too self-confident? He certainly has a good try at laying down his life for Jesus. A whole contingent of armed police arrives in Gethsemane to arrest Jesus. They are well armed, because they expect there might be resistance. Jesus has eleven disciples with him – or perhaps a few more – but only two swords among them. Peter has one of the swords, and he uses it. This is not necessarily reckless. Jesus might have been able to escape in the dark while Peter and the others kept the police busy. Jesus might have survived, and Peter might have lost his life saving him. If only Jesus had let him.

Instead Jesus says (and Peter has to obey): 'Put your sword back into its sheath. Am I not to drink the cup that the Father has given me?'

So Peter proves courageous. He risks his own life in devotion to Jesus. The trouble is that he's got Jesus and discipleship all wrong. He wants Jesus to be the Messiah the way he, Peter, thinks Jesus should be the Messiah, and he wants to be the sort of disciple he, Peter, thinks the Messiah should have. He wants Jesus to take the obvious way to success and achievement. He wants to be Jesus' right-hand man, playing a big part in his success. He will even risk his life for the sake of Jesus' survival and success. What he cannot appreciate – but who can blame him, that side of the cross? – is Jesus' extraordinary, chosen route to success only through failure, his path to achievement only through loss. Peter would do anything to save Jesus *from* the cross, but he cannot accompany Jesus on the way to the cross.

Therefore, once forbidden by Jesus to use his sword, Peter, with the other disciples, takes flight. He was prepared to save Jesus, but if Jesus insists on not being saved, there is nothing he can do. Even so Peter proves more devoted to Jesus than the others, more courageous than the others. He follows, say the Gospels, at a distance. A disillusioned disciple. A disciple of a failed Messiah. But still enough of a disciple to follow, at a reasonably safe distance. Still enough of a disciple to hang around in the courtyard of the high priest's house hoping for news of what happens to Jesus. Jesus, after all, is not just an idea for Peter or just a cause he wanted to see succeed. Jesus is the person he is devoted to. Jesus is the one he still wishes to follow, even in failure and even though he can no longer understand him at all.

But it is at this point that Peter himself fails. Is he simply scared, as most people reading the story assume? Does he not want to be associated with Jesus for fear he too will be arrested? Or is it also that he does not want to be associated with a failed messiah? Is he embarrassed to admit to being a follower of this man people had thought might be the Messiah but who is now so obviously not the Messiah? Maybe the talk around the fire was of other failed messiahs. There had been some: impostors who promised their followers the kingdom and the glory, only to be easily and ignominiously crushed by the Romans. Maybe they were saying, Jesus was obviously another of these, even more quickly and easily exposed as a failure. Peter fails Jesus because he cannot allow himself to be seen as the disciple of a failed messiah. Because he can still see Jesus only in terms of the way he, Peter, wants Jesus to be the Messiah, because he can still see discipleship only as helping Jesus succeed and sharing in Jesus' success, Peter fails miserably. Though he follows further than the others among the Twelve, though he shows more courage and devotion than any of them, he fails the more abjectly in the end. Because he cannot accept the cross, he cannot follow Jesus on the way to the cross.

Now we can see, surely, that Peter's failure is tremendously hopeful. It is the failure of Peter's whole misconception of Jesus and discipleship. It is the shattering of all Peter's illusions about Jesus and himself. It is the one way in which Peter's remarkable devotion to Jesus can be remade into true discipleship. It is the only way Peter can stop thinking Jesus needs Peter to help him succeed the way Peter wants him to. It is the only way Peter can begin to see instead that it is Peter who needs Jesus to enable him to be a disciple the way Jesus wants him to be. It is the only way Peter can find God's grace in the crucified Messiah and be able to follow Jesus on the way of the cross himself.

Peter's failure qualifies him to begin to be a disciple on the way of the cross. Only by falling can Peter be raised up. His failure is God's success. This is one of those paradoxes to which the way of the cross always leads. Jesus dies that we might have life. Only by losing ourselves do we find ourselves. Only by giving up can we succeed. It is not just that the cross – Jesus' winning by losing, succeeding by failing, living through dying – is the prime example of these paradoxes. The cross itself creates all these paradoxes. In Jesus' failure, condemnation and death, God meets us all in our failure, our condemnation, our death, in order to create for us the new beginning

that is in reality our first true beginning after all our false starts.
Peter's false start at discipleship ran irretrievably into the ground in
the high priest's courtyard as Jesus was being condemned to death.
And as Jesus looked at Peter, as Jesus on his way to the cross looked
at Peter at the point of Peter's abject failure, as the failed Messiah
looking at the failed disciple, there on the way to the cross Peter's new
beginning as a disciple began.

To realize what a new beginning it was, we may remember that
thirty-five years later Peter was quite literally to follow Jesus on the
way of the cross, carrying his own cross out through the gates of the
city of Rome to be crucified himself. As Jesus said to him at the Last
Supper: 'Where I am going, you cannot follow me now; but you will
follow afterward.'

Two aspects of the way Peter's failure proves to be his salvation
deserve our attention. First, there is that shattering of illusions. It is
not that Peter slips up and can then pick himself up again and go on.
Peter got Jesus completely wrong and discipleship completely wrong.
He cannot just pick up where he left off. He can only start again on
a wholly new and different basis. The illusion that Peter, with his
courage, his initiative and his devotion to Jesus, can save Jesus from
death, be Jesus' greatest disciple, and make sure Jesus succeeds, has
been dispelled. Instead Peter must see that, for *all* his courage, his
initiative and his devotion to Jesus, he cannot be a disciple at all
unless Jesus dies for him. Instead of the illusion that Jesus needs him,
he must know that in the first place it is he who needs Jesus. And the
Jesus he needs is not his imagined Jesus, the Jesus he would die for,
but the real Jesus, the Jesus who died for him, the Jesus whose way to
the cross is the way of God's grace most especially for failures.

The cross shatters our illusions. It shatters our illusions about
ourselves. It shatters our illusions about Jesus. It shatters our illusions about the world. Jesus, we discover, is not there to fulfill our
aspirations, however fine they may be. Jesus does not conform to the
world's aspirations, however attractive they may seem. Jesus does not

confirm our self-made images of ourselves, the way we like to think of ourselves, the way we would like others to think of us. There is no smooth path to God which we can ascend with all our expectations of life confirmed and fulfilled. There is only the way of the cross, where the condemned and crucified Jesus contradicts our expectations, forces us to see ourselves as we really are, not as we would like to be seen, and reveals the world as a strange new landscape we had not seen before, a paradoxical game in which only losers can succeed.

The dispelling of illusions can be painful, but it can also be a great relief, and it is always liberating. For the other key aspect of what happens to Peter is simply the discovery that failure is not at all a disqualification for being a disciple of Jesus. On the contrary, failure is a qualification for being a disciple of Jesus. There are not only the big dramatic failures, like Peter's, but also the little, everyday failures and the accumulating failures that add up to the despairing sense that we never get any better, never manage to follow Jesus more faithfully.

But our failure is God's opportunity, the point where God's grace always proves to be greater. We may have to learn, like Peter, that it is our way rather than God's we are pursuing. How could we ever learn that if we found nothing but success in following our own way? It may be our self-confidence in our own abilities that has to be dispelled. Or (because some of us are quite unlike Peter in this respect) we may harbor an opposite kind of illusion: a negative view of ourselves, an exaggerated self-denigration that inhibits our lives. What we should learn through failure is to surrender to God's grace everything we are, abilities and inabilities, expectations and aspirations, for God's grace to remake, for God to heal and to restore and to renew. Failure qualifies us for discipleship when in failure we find God to be the gracious God and ourselves to be in need of God's grace.

All of Peter's fine qualities were not, of course, wasted. They were not left aside in Peter's new beginning. But they had to be yielded to God before they could be used by God. Even Peter's willingness to die for Jesus had to be yielded to God. It had to become the willingness

to die for the Jesus who had first died for Peter. Peter did become
what Jesus had all along known he would be — the foremost shepherd
of Jesus' flock — but only through failure and only on the far side of
the cross.

For Prayer & Reflection

Lord Jesus,
too often we want to be
your disciples in our own way,
not yours;
too often we want you
to endorse our projects
and give them success;
too often we pursue
our own very worthy objectives;
instead of following you
on your way to the cross.

Forgive us.

Dispel our illusions
as we see you
in the world's eyes a failure,
condemned, mocked,
suffering, dead.

Restore and renew us.

Help us to surrender ourselves to God,
what we can and cannot do,

our failures and our achievements,
our hopes and aspirations.
Help us to leave success to God
desiring only to follow where you lead.

In your way to the cross
we find God's grace to us
in our failure,
grace always greater than our failure.

Accept us again as disciples
who would live for you and die for you,
who can live for you and die for you,
because you have died and live for us.

As you said again to Peter
when, risen again, you spoke to him
of his continuing love for you,
so you say to us:
'Follow me.'

He Went Out and Wept Bitterly

The cock crows and Peter remembers Jesus' words:
'Before the cock crows you will deny me three times.'
And he went out and wept bitterly.
I wonder what Peter was weeping about.
It was not for you that he wept.
Your situation was no better or worse.
You were going to die.
Peter had come to see the end.

Why the bitter tears?
The bitter tears were for Peter.
The bitter tears were for the death of the old Peter.
Peter the strong
Peter the true
Peter the man in charge
His tears were for the death of Peter in control;
Peter on top of things
Peter the man of integrity
Peter the faithful friend
Peter the afraid-of-nobody
Peter the superior to his weak brothers
These were all self-images very dear to Peter.
He had depended on them for the meaning of his life.
Those were the things that made him special, different, admirable.
In one moment of clarity
he saw they were not the real Peter
The real Peter was the one who to protect himself
would deny with a curse even knowing a friend he
had sworn to stand by to the death.
His tears were tears of mourning for his lost self-esteem.
It was a terrible loss.
He wept bitterly.

In charge. On top of things. Integrity. Courage.
I try to be like that, Lord.
Most of the time I'm pretty good at it.
I bear my share around the house, around the office.
I work very hard. People depend on me.
Sometimes I'm tough, but I am reasonable.
I get a lot done.
Sometimes I have bad luck, or I take a job too big for me, and things
don't work out the way I like.

But I'm a fair man. I don't ask anyone to do something I wouldn't do
myself.

That's the way I am. Or that's the way I thought I was.

Last week my secretary quit because she said, I was thoughtless and
unreasonable.

She was a good secretary. I didn't want to lose her.

I don't know what happened.

I thought she knew I appreciated her.

I gave her raises when I could. I took her out to lunch now and then.

I know I criticized her work sometimes, and even lost my temper with
her,

but that's part of the job.

My work gets criticized – more often and less fairly.

She said I was a sexist.

that I didn't respect her as a person

or treat her as an equal.

I couldn't believe it. I thought she must be getting her period.

When I got home, I got no sympathy from my wife.

She said my secretary was right and launched into a diatribe about
how thoughtless I was at home,

how neglectful of her and the children,

how bossy and authoritarian I had become.

She went on and on, and as she talked everything I believed about
myself began to come apart: the kind of man I was, the kind of father
I was, the kind of employer I was – it was all eroded by the acid of her
tongue.

Suddenly I knew that deep down somewhere in this woman I loved
there was a pool of hurt and anger I had never glimpsed.

I had hurt her.

But I didn't understand how I had done it.

Or how I could be different.

I began to cry.

She began to cry.

I reached out to her. She held me. I held her.
We really do love each other.
But where do we go from here?
Is there a life for us beyond this death?

I see you speaking to Peter beside another charcoal fire.
I see you speaking to him by the sea where he earned his living.
I see you coming back to him when he thought you were gone.
Asking him one question, over and over, as if it were all that mattered.

Do you love me? Feed my sheep.
Do you love me? Feed my sheep.
Do you love me? Feed my sheep.

You offered him a new life in place of the old Peter who had died.

I am waiting Lord. Come by me, Lord.

Reid Isaac

4

CAIAPHAS:

THE MAN WHO COULDN'T LIVE WITH JESUS

Readings: Matthew 26:57–68; John 11:45–53

No doubt Caiaphas would have preferred not to have to deal with Jesus at all; but like many others before and since he had little choice in the matter. Caiaphas was high priest in the year that Jesus made the headlines in Jerusalem, and this job gave him responsibility for political and civil as well as religious affairs within Palestine. He was a sort of archbishop and prime minister rolled into one. Technically all that he did was under the jurisdiction of the occupying Roman forces. Within these formal limits, though, Caiaphas enjoyed a fair amount of power and a set of responsibilities sufficient to keep even the most organized person occupied for more hours than there were in the day. This was not an easy job, but it was one which Caiaphas apparently enjoyed and was good at; historical sources tell us that he held it for thirty years. This was unusual. Most people served for a few years and then either threw in the towel, allowing younger and more energetic colleagues to assume the burden of office, or fell into disfavor with the Romans and found themselves suddenly 'retiring in order to spend more time with my family.' But Caiaphas stuck at it. No matter how much satisfaction his job gave him, though, there can have been few points in his long and distinguished career that caused Caiaphas more headaches than did this particular Passover festival.

Passover was always difficult for the Jewish establishment. Jerusalem was packed to the gunwales with pilgrims from all over the known world, crowds pulsing with expectation and hope, their minds full of the ancient Passover themes of divine deliverance from slavery and the gift to Israel of the Promised Land. In this season the Roman occupation of Palestine stuck in the throats of most Jews even more than usual. The atmosphere in the city streets was thickly coated with hope, and every other casual conversation was seasoned with talk of the Messiah and when God would at last send him. It was an effective powder keg, just waiting for a spark to ignite it. The danger every year was that some fanatic or other would seize the moment, taking the opportunity to whip the crowds into an anti-Roman frenzy that could result only in terrible bloodshed and a heavy-handed clampdown.

For Caiaphas and his colleagues in the Sanhedrin life under the Romans was no bed of roses, but it could be worse. It was their perpetual task to try and ensure that nothing happened to make it worse. These men were charged with the unenviable task of balancing the delicate concerns of Israel's national and religious identity with the political realities of life as an outpost of the Roman Empire. It was a balance all too easily upset. The task called on occasion for a sensible dose of *realpolitik*; and it's no surprise to learn that Caiaphas had been heard to say that if and when the situation demanded it, it would be legitimate that one man should be sacrificed for the good of the nation as a whole.

Passover, then, was a major headache for the high priest and the Jewish authorities every year. This year looked to be no exception. The arrival of Jesus in Jerusalem on the previous Sunday heralded by crowds of palm-waving and slogan-shouting groupies augured ill for a trouble-free festival. Caiaphas had to decide how he was going to handle the situation.

What made Jesus such a threat and brought him eventually to trial before the Sanhedrin? If we read through the Gospels we begin to see what it was. From the outset of his ministry we find Jesus doing and saying things that set him in immediate, apparent conflict with those who wanted above all to maintain the status quo in Jewish life. He challenged the established orthodoxies both tacitly and explicitly. He broke the Jewish law, or at least insisted on interpreting it in ways which didn't fit in with accepted ways of thinking and behaving, so that one of the earliest reactions to him was the persistent questioning of the Pharisees: How come you and your disciples don't fast at the prescribed times? Why do you break the sabbath law, healing the sick on a day of rest? And so on. Jesus taught, the crowds began to say, with an innate authority, the sort of authority that compels people to listen and is self-authenticating. Much of what he had to say was openly critical of the religious establishment. His words, however novel and surprising they may have been to Jewish ears, had a ring of truth about them, not, as people soon began to observe, like the words of the scribes and teachers of the law.

Jesus' actions backed up his words and formed a powerful unity with them. If what Jesus said was dangerously unorthodox and provocative, could it nonetheless not be dismissed as the novel ranting of a self-styled prophet or messiah – good for entertainment but with no lasting or damaging effects? Had this option been open to Caiaphas and his henchmen it might have been an attractive one. But Jesus had not styled himself any such thing. His ministry was remarkably free from the razzmatazz of self-publicity. He did what he did and said what he said, and let other people worry about finding labels to stick on him.

Yet his presence in the city and among the people was electric and could hardly be ignored or dismissed. Jesus' words burned with authority, and his ministry of healing and restoring people's lives furnished a tangible word that pointed to an unavoidable conclusion. There was something special, something outside the normal run of cranks and quacks and peddlers of religious enthusiasm whose trade fed mercilessly on the attentions of the desperate and the gullible. There was no blatant self-aggrandizement, no all too willing acceptance of the people's adulation and money on the part of Jesus and his disciples. Rather there was an unnerving aspect to all that Jesus did and said, an aspect that refused to be accounted for in purely human terms, one that pointed, albeit obliquely and indirectly, to the presence of God's kingdom (i.e., of God's own power and rule) in his person and activity.

No wonder the people were amazed. No wonder they continually asked questions about who he was. No wonder Jesus was the main topic of conversation wherever he went. Nothing he did or said would have mattered if he had been an oddball of whom no serious notice was being taken. But the crowds followed him wherever he went – out of curiosity at first and then in the conviction that he was someone worth hearing, worth being near. After all, you never knew just what might happen when Jesus was around. The things he did and said attracted attention, even though Jesus himself frequently sought to escape undue publicity and notice. 'Go,' he told people, 'and say nothing of this to anyone.' But he might as well have saved his breath. In the coffee bars, the supermarkets, the tennis clubs and the polite dinner parties of Palestine from Nazareth to Jerusalem the name of Jesus was on everyone's lips.

This was the man who arrived in the city of Jerusalem just before the Passover festival. And now, having had the gall to come into the lion's den of religious establishment, Jesus refused to tone down his provocative and potentially disruptive behavior. Indeed it seemed as if he were determined to step it up until the collision of interests and authority became inevitable. He waltzed into the temple and began to cause a public fray, claiming that this bastion of the ancient Jewish religion was corrupt and, worse still, that *he* had the authority to purge it; that it was, in some sense, *his* to cleanse. Having driven out the traders and moneychangers from the temple courts, Jesus sat down and began to heal the lame and the blind and little children ran around noisily shouting, 'Hosanna to the Son of David.' It's hardly surprising that, as Matthew tells us, the chief priests and teachers of the law were indignant. On the face of it they had good reason to be. 'Where do you get your authority from?' they asked him. But Jesus refused to answer them directly. He left them to work it out for themselves.

What had Caiaphas said? 'It is better for you to have one man die for the people than to have the whole nation destroyed.' And John's Gospel expands his thinking for us. 'If we let this man go on like this,' Caiaphas reasoned, 'everyone will believe in him, and then the Romans will come and destroy both our holy place and our nation.' In other words, to let Jesus continue was to risk some sort of popular nationalistic and religious outburst in the city. If this happened the Romans would almost certainly take direct action to crush it and dismantle the Sanhedrin and perhaps even destroy the temple, thereby effectively removing the locus of Jewish national and religious identity and opposition. And so, Mark's Gospel tells us, 'they kept looking for a way to kill him; for they were afraid of him' (Mk 11:18). Jesus was too dangerous, too provocative, too popular to be ignored. The only way to deal with him was to be rid of him. That might involve some unpleasant and less than strictly by-the-book dealings, some strong nerves and malleable consciences, but it was necessary for the sake of national security and the good of the people. Jesus must go.

That's how this group of seventy-one respectable Jewish men, religious leaders, teachers, members of the business community, politicians, come to be gathered furtively in Caiaphas's home so late at night for a hurried and urgently convened meeting. They desperately scratch around for evidence that might give their actions a veneer of acceptability and integrity. They send out the temple guard to arrest Jesus and drag him to a kangaroo court when the crowds are asleep in their hotels and guest houses. It's a sordid scenario, and one that gets worse as, intoxicated by the urgency and the need for assurance of the rightness of their chosen course of action, those present begin first to demonize Jesus and then, as so often happens, to feel free to abuse and to dehumanize him with violence and mockery.

Yet Caiaphas, with whom the responsibility for this whole episode would finally rest, had never sought this conflict or the messy circumstances to which it had led. He would have been much happier if Jesus had taken the hint and tempered his words and behavior when first challenged. But he didn't. Jesus saw the likely outcome of his own actions, yet he persisted in them, refusing to compromise, refusing to play the game on terms laid down by others, remaining faithful to what he understood his task to be. What choice did Caiaphas have? What else could he have done in the circumstances? What would we have done?

Jesus can be a surprising, an inconvenient and even an uncomfortable person to meet and to deal with. For when Jesus comes to us he does so on his terms, not on ours. What he stands for and embodies in his life and ministry so often directly challenges and even contradicts our ways of thinking about ourselves, our neighbors, our responsibilities before God, our values and priorities. What we deem important and set such store by he treats as of little matter. Our attempts to impress and to persuade him of our worth make no apparent impression upon him, not that he ignores or bypasses us. (Sometimes we find ourselves wishing secretly that he would – the sentiment expressed in Augustine's famous prayer, 'O Lord, save me, but not yet.')

Jesus' sensibilities and values seem to be tuned to a different wavelength from ours, and the process of retuning ours is far from easy or comfortable. He comes into our crowded Jerusalem and insists on purging the citadel of our religious life of its trash and clutter and corruption. Until he has done so he can do little or nothing with us or for us. He offers to heal and restore the sickness and blindness in our lives but finds us indignant rather than willing, afraid rather than joyful. We fear the possible costs to ourselves and our way of living and understanding if we abandon ourselves to the claims that he makes upon us and so find ourselves changing. We resent his blunt refusal to negotiate, to work out a compromise between his lordship and the many other claims laid upon us in this life. So often when he comes we try to ignore him, to dismiss him, to sideline him. But before long we find that he persists and that his claim upon us confronts us wherever we look, facing us squarely with alternative ways of doing and seeing things that make us uncomfortable as we continue in our normal compromise with the world. Instead of welcoming him gladly, granting him a triumphal entry into our lives, we do as Caiaphas and his henchmen did. We wait until the opportunity, the dark moment arises, and then we seek to put him to death for the sake of a quiet and peaceful existence.

For Prayer & Reflection

Lord Jesus,
like Caiaphas there are times when we would prefer
not to have to deal with you.

Sensing your uninvited approach
we rush to make our excuses:
Not today, Lord.

Things are too difficult just now,
too delicate,
too complicated.

We want you to come only on our terms.
We want you to reinforce our ways of thinking and behaving,
 to endorse and lend your support to our plans
for bringing in the kingdom of God.

But when you come to us
it is always on your terms and not ours.
You quietly but firmly insist.
No negotiation.
No diplomatic compromises.
Just faithful correspondence to the Father's bidding.

And so you upset the carefully arranged apple carts of our lives.
And so you leave us with little choice.
We cannot ignore you.

Forgive us for the times when, like Caiaphas,
we have reckoned the cost of accommodating you to be too great.
And so flood our lives with your Spirit
that when you come to us again
we shall be ready to welcome you with open arms
putting ourselves,
our plans,
our priorities
and not you
on the cross.

Amen.

5

PONTIUS PILATE:

THE MAN WHO COULDN'T MAKE UP HIS MIND

Readings: Luke 23:1–25; John 18:28–19:16

What sort of man was Pontius Pilate? Ostensibly he was a power-ful man. As prefect of the Roman province of Judaea he had at his disposal considerable military force, and in theory he mediated Rome's control over this occupied territory. Formally no one did any-thing without his permission.

In particular Pilate was the only one with authority to have Jesus put to death. The Jews were allowed to exercise their traditional religious and civil code of law on a devolved level of authority but only within clearly defined limits. One thing they were not permitted to do was to sentence anyone to death, let alone execute that sentence. This sanction was one that Rome preferred to keep within its own hands. If Caiaphas wanted to have Jesus executed, then he had to persuade Pilate that such a course of action was in the obvious interests of the empire or of Pilate – or both.

On the face of it, then, Pilate was a powerful man indeed, propped up by all the weight that the imperial might of Rome could afford. He held the keys of life and death in his hands. The vital decision in this story of Jesus' passion was his alone to make. Everything depended on his judgment.

Yet the irony of the story as it is told in the Gospels is that Pilate emerges as perhaps the weakest of all the characters. He is skillfully and relatively easily manipulated by Caiaphas, who presents Jesus to him not as a blasphemer (what did Rome care about the religious prejudices and squabbles of the locals?) but as a messianic pretender, a potential threat to Roman government, a dangerous political insurgent. In the story Pilate may be weak but he's certainly not stupid, and even he can see that this claim is far fetched. We can almost hear the tone of bemused incredulity in his question to Jesus: 'Are *you* the king of the Jews?' Although the Gospels betray little interest in the physical appearance of Jesus, it is reasonable to suppose that he hardly looked the part of a dangerous guerilla leader. As Jesus points out to Pilate in John's version of events, unlike the zealots his followers carry no weapons, and there has been no rioting, not even any protest, in the wake of his arrest. Those who had been with him for three years had all alike sought the camouflage and anonymity of the crowd at the first sign of danger. No matter what this man may have been saying about himself, in real terms the threat offered by Jesus to Roman authority and the stability of civil order hardly registers on Pilate's scale.

But at this crucial juncture in the plot, Pilate's personal weakness and political vulnerability are laid bare. 'If you release this man,' says Caiaphas quietly, '*you* are no friend of the emperor.' With these few words he binds Pilate completely.

Like so many people in positions of political power Pilate is a man with a past that haunts him, an Achilles heel that occasionally forces him to limp. And as Caiaphas utters those carefully chosen words, locking Pilate deliberately in his gaze as he does so, the Achilles heel begins to twinge.

There had been occasions when Pilate had been tactless in his dealings with the Jews, and those occasions had eventually cost him more than he cared to remember in terms of political profile and career prospects. He had taken money from the temple treasury to finance the building of waterworks in Jerusalem. As he saw it, this was a reasonable executive action, diverting funds from local government to pay for local services. Why on earth should the money come from Rome when it was the Jews who would benefit? But Pilate, like others before him, had underestimated Jewish sensitivities where the Temple was concerned. There were riots. In dealing with these Pilate decided that he had to lay down a few ground rules about how Judaea was going to function under his jurisdiction, so he sent his troops into the city to teach the mob a brutal lesson. The resultant bloodbath had not been something to be proud of. Luke speaks with powerful irony of Pilate having mixed the blood of the crowds with that of the temple sacrifices (Lk 13:1). Even the troops had found little pleasure in beating up unarmed civilians. There was no glory in it.

Then there had been the matter of his men using shields bearing an image of the emperor Tiberius. The Jews viewed these as highly offensive and had complained, pointing out that, so far as their religion was concerned, it was idolatrous for such images to be borne into the temple precincts. They requested that imageless shields be used instead. But Pilate, determined to make his mark as a strong governor tolerating no nonsense, stood his ground. A Roman soldier's kit was standard issue, and he wasn't going to modify it to satisfy some superstition. This time there had been no riots. Instead the Jews appealed directly to Tiberius Caesar, complaining that the behavior of his local representative was immoderate and unreasonable, and cast the empire in a poor light. This was a risky strategy. If Tiberius were minded to back Pilate's actions, then, humanly speaking at least, there was no higher court of appeal, and things could look bleak and become uncomfortable for those who had dared to question Roman authority.

But Tiberius had proved to be a better judge of political realities than had his ambassador, and he forced Pilate to make a very public U-turn in policy. It was a decision that effectively undermined Pilate's authority from there on. He knew and the Jewish authorities knew (and he knew that the Jewish authorities knew!) that Tiberius would be unlikely to tolerate another embarrassing misdemeanor. Pilate's career had just reached its summit: any more trouble under his jurisdiction and it would be over altogether!

With this in view, those words of Caiaphas come highly charged. So often in human power games what is left unsaid rather than what is said really matters. 'If you release this man, you are no friend of the emperor.' Pilate has all the armed might of Rome theoretically at his fingertips, yet his hands are tied by his history of political misjudgment and Caiaphas's willingness to exploit it. In theory Pilate is free to spoil Caiaphas's plans for Jesus. (And how he must long to do just that!) Yet in practice he knows that this man must die; otherwise *he* will have to pay the political price. Integrity does not come cheap, and Pilate can't afford it.

Although Pilate does all he can to persuade the Jews to let Jesus go, they insist. And Pilate, the demands of conscience and justice notwithstanding, surrenders Jesus to their will. His final maneuver is to avoid being seen to have made any decision at all. He tries to convince himself and the crowds that he is neutral in this affair, that he is lending no aid to the cause of those who want Jesus put to death. He literally washes his hands of the situation, trying in vain to cleanse them of the blood with which they are in effect already drenched, seeking absolution for a sin he cannot bring himself to own. Politicians down the ages since have frequently discovered that responsibility is less easily sluiced away than this. It is perhaps a fitting irony that Pilate's sin of complicity in political murder has been publicly remembered in Christian liturgy since the earliest times: 'crucified under Pontius Pilate.' It can hardly be the way any civil servant would want his career to go down in history.

Are we not sometimes like Pilate in our dealings with Jesus? We find ourselves confronted with an unlooked for and unwelcome encounter with him. Face to face we find ourselves intrigued by his claims, recognizing that there is something different, something special about him that we cannot pin down. We feel the force of his demand on our energies, our time, our loyalties, our lives. Perhaps we feel compelled in spite of ourselves to take our stand with him against the crowd and the world. But counting the cost of doing so we find it to be too high. So, rather than turning him away or trying to put him to death we seek instead to make our excuses, to withdraw from the situation, to adopt a morally noncommittal if uncomfortable neutrality. We try to defer the moment, to put the decision on ice. But it didn't work for Pilate, and it won't work for us.

For Prayer & Reflection

Holy Father,
you sent your Son into the world
to be our Judge
and thereby our Redeemer.

His life of perfect sonship
exposes the madness and prodigal waste
of our continual bid to escape your holy love.

We prefer to set our own standards,
determine our own values,

frame a pattern for our own lives,
be our own judge.

Like Pilate,
confronted with the scandal of Jesus' weakness and humility,
we sense the true meaning of kingship
yet find it difficult to take our stand with him.
The forces of the world ensnare us.

Help us never to seek to wash our hands of him,
but make us as firm in our commitment to him
as he is in his commitment to us.

Amen.

6

BARABBAS:

A CLOSE SCRAPE WITH DEATH

Readings: Mark 15:6–15; John 18:38–40

We are not told much about Barabbas in the Gospels. He is one of those minor characters who enters and then leaves the stage quickly as a sort of extra to the main action being played out on it. Significant only for the way in which his story crosses and weaves together momentarily with Jesus' own, Barabbas doesn't even have any lines to say. So it's not too surprising that the Evangelists don't elaborate on either his history or his character. To do so not only would be surplus to the strict requirements of their purpose but also might distract the reader from what really matters. Jesus, we might surmise, was to prove to be a far more significant player in Barabbas's

story than Barabbas was in Jesus'. The Gospel writers are concerned
with the latter. We, though, may profitably dwell on what little we
know of Barabbas and imagine some of what we are not told about
this man and his fleeting 'nonencounter' with Jesus, a man whom he
had never actually met but whose life and fate had now become
impossible to disentangle from his own.

Barabbas is described by John as a *lestes*, a bandit. Paul (1 Cor
11:26) uses the same word to describe the thugs who would lie in wait
for travelers in the ancient world and then swoop on them, demand-
ing not so much their money or their lives as very likely both! Maybe
Barabbas had been mixed up with this sort of organized crime. But
there was more to it than this.

The other three Gospels tell us that he was a *stasiastes*, one who
had been involved in a recent political insurrection and had committed murder in the process. This locates Barabbas among a group
within Jewish society whose shadowy lifestyle blurred the boundaries
between crime and politics. Disaffected by the collaboration of the
Jewish authorities with imperial government, these rebels looked for
opportunities to disadvantage the Romans wherever and whenever
they arose and no matter what means must be embraced to further
the end. To call Barabbas an insurrectionist or a rebel does not
contradict John's description so much as sketch in a bit of the detail
for us. Those whose lives are dedicated to violent causes and violent
means are often driven to embrace a wider pattern of criminal existence to fund their activities. Barabbas and his sort, forced outside
the normal economic and domestic structures, would likely have
resorted to indiscriminate mugging and armed robbery in order to
keep body and soul together. They were desperate men with a desperate mission and were prepared to go to desperate lengths to see it
realized.

We should not submit to the temptation to romanticize a man
such as Barabbas. The truism that 'one person's terrorist is another's
freedom fighter' has its limits and ought not to be allowed to dissolve

moral black and white into a myriad of shades of gray. Whatever the truth may be about Barabbas's descent into a life of crime and violence, whatever his higher motives may have been, we are dealing with a brigand and a murderer, not a first-century Robin Hood.

It is nonetheless easy to see how Barabbas might have possessed a sort of rough charm that would commend him to the crowds in this Passover season. Many of them shared his political sentiments in broad outline, even if they did not condone his methods or the lifestyle that fueled them and that placed the lives of ordinary, innocent Palestinians at risk. In the heat of the political moment it was easy for them to overlook the crime and the violence and for Barabbas to become a convenient symbol of anti-Roman sympathies. Pilate's obvious preference for Jesus over Barabbas may have been sufficient in itself to engender such mass moral myopia and to sway the crowd quickly behind the call to 'free the "Jerusalem One!"'

What is remarkable is the way in which Caiaphas and the Jewish authorities orchestrated this campaign and whipped the festival crowd into such a frenzy that Pilate could hardly have resisted their demands without precipitating another revolt. After all, to them Barabbas and his kind were an embarrassment; worse, these insurrectionists were a serious risk to whatever self-determination and religious freedom Rome allowed the Jews to exercise. How many more grisly acts of terror by these misguided zealots would the empire tolerate before losing patience and turning Palestine into a police state? And they could have been under few illusions about their own likely fate were such thugs ever to bump into them alone and unprotected. For all sorts of reasons the efficient capture and despatching of men like Barabbas by the forces of Roman justice was something to which the Jewish leaders had every reason to lend tacit support. Yet they conspired to have *this man* rather than Jesus released! This is indicative, surely, of just how far their resentment against and their fear of Jesus had actually come.

How much did Barabbas know of Jesus? As he left his cell and joined the crowds on the streets of Jerusalem, how much did he grasp of what he owed to this man whom injustice had thrust onto the gibbet in his place? Did he try to find out, to understand, to make sense of what had happened? Did he loiter for a while, curious to watch and to see Jesus' story through to its bitter end? Or did he make a sharp exit, taking no risks and fearing possible rearrest on some trumped-up charge? Perhaps he left the city on the Emmaus road, passing the foot of the hill called Golgotha. If so, did he pause and look up and see what they were doing to this man in his place? Had he done so, what effect might it have had on him, this calloused spirit with so much blood on his own hands? What, if anything, would he have felt? Relief? Pity? Regret? Shame? Or indifference?

Perhaps Barabbas simply saw his chance for freedom and took it without asking too many questions. Jesus' life in exchange for his: it was an efficient transaction from his point of view, and the time for anguished reflection about the fairness or the meaning of it was later — if ever. For the present all he could be expected to do was to accept his circumstance with pragmatism and try to put the smell of death (which had hung around him for days and had soaked deep into his soul) as far behind him as he could. After all, Barabbas could do nothing to change things even if he had wanted to. No one was asking his opinion. He didn't invite Jesus to take his place. Someone else had made all the relevant decisions, and he was glad to grasp the unexpected and undeserved chance being offered to him.

Maybe, though, as he paused to catch his breath once he was convinced that no one was pursuing him, he might reflect on the oddity of it all. How absurd that he, of all people, should be not only alive but also set free from the burden that his messy and complex past had hung around his neck. It was 3 o'clock in the afternoon. By rights he should have been breathing his last just about now. Instead he could do what he liked. An imperial pardon was an imperial pardon, and it looked as if this time there were no catches. If ever there was such a thing as the chance for a fresh start in this life, then this was it. He

supposed that in a strange sort of way he had Jesus to thank for that.
Funny the way things work out in this world! He wondered how Jesus
must have felt about things; forced to swap places with the scum of
society and getting mixed up with a mess that he didn't have any part
in making? He should have played his cards with Pilate better: given
the right answers, stroked his political ego, even groveled a bit if that
was what it took. He could have escaped, a little the worse for being
detained at the pleasure of the Roman Empire ('the prisoner sus-
tained his injuries being apprehended during an attempted escape')
but with his life intact. But then he, Barabbas, would be there, hanging lifeless on the cross instead of Jesus, rather than here, with an
open future ahead of him and wondering just what to do with the rest
of a life he hadn't expected to have.

For Prayer & Reflection

Barabbas was sitting in his dark and dirty cell, listening carefully to
the crowds milling around in the courtyard outside. There was more
noise than usual today. He was sitting and waiting: waiting for the
time, not far off now, when the guards would come to fetch him and
take him to begin the last journey he would ever make.

From outside the city walls the sound of hammering and sawing
could already be heard clearly as local tradesmen, chatting and joking
among themselves, toiled to construct the awful machinery of capital
punishment.

Of course he deserved what was coming. He had deprived others
of life, and according to Roman law his just desert lay in the impale-
ment of his own life on the gibbet. Even so, he could hardly bring
himself to think about what lay ahead. He had seen men crucified
before. He had seen the fear and the agony etched in their faces; and
he knew that it could take a very long time to die. Although he didn't

like to admit it, even to himself, he was scared, not of death but of this particular way of dying. There was no glory in crucifixion, only humiliation and mockery. He just hoped he could summon enough willpower at the last to deny the crowd the satisfaction of a broken and whimpering victim. If only things had worked out differently . . . Now, though, it was too late for pondering what might have been. Today Barabbas was to be punished for his crimes. Today 'justice' would be done.

Outside the crowds were getting excited. Barabbas wondered what could be causing so much fuss. An hour or so ago they had taken Jesus, a carpenter from Nazareth, outside for his trial. Jesus had raised some eyebrows by speaking out against the Jewish authorities; but, so far as Barabbas knew, he hadn't committed any serious crime. Of course he would be humiliated, perhaps given a savage beating to keep the crowds happy, and then released back into the obscurity from which he had come.

The yelling of the crowds grew ever louder. Barabbas couldn't hear everything, but the few phrases he did manage to pick out froze his blood: 'We want Barabbas!' 'Crucify him! Crucify him!' This is it, he thought to himself. *Not long now and it will all be over.*

There were footsteps approaching outside in the corridor. Barabbas felt his stomach muscles tense involuntarily and a sudden nausea overwhelm him as the bolts of the cell door were drawn back. As the door opened he muttered a quick prayer under his breath. Old habits refused to die.

What happened next took several minutes to sink in. Surely there must be some mistake. He repeated the guard's words to himself: 'All right, Barabbas, you can go. You're a free man. Don't ask me why, but they're going to crucify Jesus of Nazareth instead of you.'

7

SIMON OF CYRENE:

CARRYING THE
CROSS

Reading: Mark 15:20–32

The standard procedure in Roman crucifixion involved vicious flogging of the victim before he was led out to the place of execution. Upright stakes were often a permanent fixture at the site, because it was in frequent use, but the victim was often required to carry the heavy wooden crossbeam that would then be fastened to the upright stake to form the cross-shape or T-shape of the scaffold to which the victim was then nailed. In Jesus' case the flogging must have led to considerable loss of blood and left him very weak already. He proved physically unable to carry the crossbeam very far. So the soldiers picked on a passer-by and obliged him to take up Jesus' cross and to carry it to the place of execution outside the city.

This is how a man called Simon of Cyrene was dragged into Jesus'
way to the cross against his will. He was not even one of the crowd
going out to see the crucifixions that day. He was going in the other
direction. He had been in the country, probably doing a day's work in
the fields, and now coming back to his home in Jerusalem. He would
not even have heard what was going on. But he could hardly be surprised at what happens to him. This is an occupied country. Roman
soldiers forcing ordinary, innocent Jews to do whatever they needed
doing for them was part of the unpleasant reality of daily life under
oppressive foreign rule.

We know nothing about Simon that Mark does not tell us in just
one verse of his Gospel. But that verse tells us a surprising amount.
Simon came from Cyrene, a city on the North African coast, in
modern Libya. The city had a large Jewish community, and Simon
was most certainly Jewish. Because he came from Africa, readers of
the Gospels have often liked to imagine Simon as black. He may have
been. A person could be both Jewish and black. Just as visitors to
Jerusalem today are sometimes surprised to see how many young
Israeli soldiers are black (because they are Ethiopian Jews, Falashas),
so there would have been some black Jews in Jerusalem in Jesus' time.
Anyone could become Jewish, and many people did. Since color pre-
judice did not exist in the ancient world, no one would have found
black faces among all the other Jewish and Gentile faces in Jerusalem
at Passover time remarkable.

Simon may have been black, but we have no way of knowing that.
We can know that he was one of those Jews who were born in the
Jewish diaspora – outside Palestine – but had returned to live in the
holy city. He is not a pilgrim visiting for the festival, like many of the
other people crowding the narrow streets of the city this week. Simon
has been out working in the fields. He lives in Jerusalem. So he is
quite familiar with the constant minor irritations and major bru-
talities of living under Roman rule in this most troublesome of the
provinces of the empire.

A final implication of Mark's one verse about Simon is that Simon became a Christian. Mark identifies him as the father of Alexander and Rufus, a pointless piece of information unless these two were Christian leaders well known to Mark's first readers. So Simon's accidental involvement with Jesus, against his will forced to carry Jesus' cross for him, somehow made him a disciple of Jesus even though he had not been one before. What did this painful accompanying of Jesus on the way to the cross do to Simon, then?

For Simon this crucifixion would initially have been different from all the others he had witnessed only because he was unlucky enough to be personally dragged into it. So it will be worth our while pausing with Simon as he takes over the burden of Jesus' cross, and viewing through Simon's eyes – typical first-century Jewish eyes – this particularly gruesome form of judicial torture and murder to which Jesus was being subjected. Crucifixion was nothing out of the ordinary in first-century Judaea. Simon would likely have seen hundreds of other crucifixion victims slowly dying this peculiarly painful form of death. Anyone in the Roman Empire would have done so, for crucifixions were frequent occurrences, but nowhere more frequent than in Jewish Palestine. Jewish resistance to the recent imposition of Roman rule was precisely the sort of crime for which this barbaric punishment was designed. Only thirty years previously no fewer than two thousand Jews had been crucified at one time outside Jerusalem, and many more since. By frequent crucifixions of criminals, slaves, dissidents and rebels, the brutal reality of Roman power was deliberately thrust in the faces of Rome's subjects: *pour encourager les autres*.

A curious fact about crucifixion is that although it was so common the Gospel narratives of the crucifixion of Jesus are actually the longest and most detailed accounts of a crucifixion we have in ancient literature. Why is it that the literature of the ancient world usually refers to crucifixion only in passing, rarely dwelling on the details? Why do so many ancient authors, who should have had occasion to refer to crucifixion, in fact avoid mentioning it at all? There

are two reasons, which can help us to put the crucifixion of Jesus in
context.

The first is that for most of the cultured, intellectual people who
wrote the literature of the ancient world, crucifixion was simply too
horrible a procedure to dwell on. It was a form of execution designed
to be as painful as possible: an excruciatingly slow death from exposure and asphyxiation, with the details of the form of execution
often improvised sadistically by the executioners. Crucifixion was
vile torture. Everyone knew that from observing it. So cultured,
literary people wanted nothing to do with it. Not that they wanted it
not to happen. They took for granted it was essential as a deterrent
to maintain civilized society. But they put it out of mind. Too much
attention to it would have disfigured their image of Roman rule as
humane and beneficent, bringing peace and prosperity to all. They
engaged in a not uncommon form of double-think. On the one hand,
they maintained an idealized picture of their society as the realm of
civilized values, while on the other hand they knew very well that the
social structure was kept in being by a system of torture and terror.
Crucifixion was in fact offensively public: it had to be to act as a
deterrent. But all the more resolutely was it banished from the literature and the culture in which the Roman Empire celebrated its
glory. Great generals like Julius Caesar, fine provincial governors like
Pliny, who regularly ordered crucifixions, wrote up their memoirs
with never a mention of the fact.

The second reason why ancient literature rarely dwells on crucifixion is that the people who got crucified were not people who
mattered. People who mattered – Roman citizens, the social elite –
could not be crucified. Crucifixion was for the lower orders, slaves
and foreigners. It was the penalty especially for crimes against the
state and for rebellious slaves. (Rebellion did not have to mean much:
the Roman poet Horace gives the example of a master who ordered
his slave's crucifixion because the slave took a surreptitious taste of
the soup while bringing it to the table.) Crucifixion maintained

Rome's political domination of a vast empire, and it maintained the structure of a slave-owning society. It was panic about slave revolts overturning all social order and panic about subject peoples like the Jews throwing off Roman rule that put thousands of people on crosses from Rome to Jerusalem.

Crucifixion was the oppressive underside of the Pax Romana, Rome's great boast of order, peace and security within the empire. Peace and prosperity for many were secured by this barbarous cruelty to others. Crucifixion was in the interests of those who enjoyed the benefits of the civilization they idealized, and it could be forgotten precisely because it was itself a way of forgetting the people who did not matter, who could be dispensed with, who paid the price for the rest of society's comfortable illusions. So that society's victims might be well and truly forgotten, crucifixion itself was not talked about.

All societies have victims, and most societies have ways of suppressing and forgetting them. Obvious examples are the torture chambers, prisons and disappearances in many a modern dictatorship, with the propaganda that cloaks them; or the mass graves of Bosnia and the conspiracies of silence that surround them. A worldwide phenomenon today is the attempt to clean up cities, making them attractive to tourists and visiting businesspeople, by removing the human eyesores – the beggars and the street children – who show them up for what they really are. Maintaining the illusion of a humane society by suppressing and forgetting its victims is a seductive process. It is a process we all need actively to resist if we are not to be self-deceived.

Perhaps we can begin to see why the gospel message of Jesus the crucified God proved so offensive to the Roman world when people like Simon of Cyrene and his sons began to preach it. A God who was executed like a political rebel or a slave. A God who was one of those victims who did not matter and ought to be forgotten. Such a God was brutally offensive, bringing to light the oppressive underside of Roman civilization, exposing the barbarism that should not be mentioned in polite conversation, assaulting the illusions of Roman society head-on. Jesus should have been one of the forgotten victims. Crucifixion should have done to him what it did to thousands of others of whom we know nothing. But in fact Jesus was remembered. The story of his crucifixion was told and retold. For two centuries Roman society tried to suppress the memory of this crucified man as it did of all others, but in this case it failed. This victim is remembered, and his solidarity with all other forgotten victims, all other victims of terror and torture, all the people who do not matter and pay the price for the comfortable illusions of the people who think they matter – Jesus' solidarity with all these brings them to remembrance too.

So what does Simon see he carries Jesus' cross to Golgotha and stays while the soldiers nail him to it? A virtually everyday scene in the Roman Empire. For a Jerusalem Jew, just one more instance of the brutal subjection that God so incomprehensibly allowed his people to suffer. Of course Jesus was one of three victims. The other two were bandits, two of those many Jews who in hard economic times, driven off their land by rents and taxation, took to the hills and formed groups of bandits, raiding the homes of the rich. They were part of the peasant resistance to the system of power and the collaboration of rich Jewish aristocrats with the Roman oppressors. They were not idealistic revolutionaries but ordinary people pushed by economic circumstances into alliance with the Jewish resistance. They were just the sort of people who got crucified, a threat to the social order as Rome perceived it. And Rome put Jesus in the same category. Jesus with the others is crushed by the need to maintain the civilized order of things as Rome defined it. The chief priests taunt him because they share the Roman view. Theirs are the interests that need victims like Jesus to preserve them.

Simon no doubt appreciates the bleak horror of crucifixion the more vividly through being dragged into it himself. He must have thought himself lucky only to have to carry a cross when so many of his countrymen died on them, like the three here. But he must also have begun to see in Jesus something that distinguished Jesus as more than just one more victim among the others.

Victim like the others he certainly was. His clothes, legitimate loot for the soldiers, are the last vestiges of human dignity stripped from him in a process of deliberate reduction to the status of absolute victim. After hours of pain, he finally cries out 'I thirst' (KJV), voicing not only the pain but the helplessness of the victim, reduced to crying for mercy to his executioners, the soldiers. His helplessness is thrown at him as a taunt by the jeering onlookers. If he dies surprisingly swiftly (some victims hung on their crosses for days), it is with the sense of total abandonment, even by his God, the victim about whom finally no one at all cares.

Jesus died in identification with the fate of all other victims, such as the two who hung beside him. He entered the darkness that many, many others have entered and still enter. Yet Jesus entered it as one who could have avoided it. He could have made his escape often in the preceding weeks and days, but he chose this way of solidarity with the victims not for his own sake but for theirs, and not for any cause of his own other than his mission to be with them and for them in love. The Gospels tell us how, hanging on the cross, Jesus was offered a narcotic to dull the pain. The women of Jerusalem, as a religious duty of compassion, used to provide execution victims with a spiced alcoholic drink to anesthetize the pain. But Jesus refused the drink. He refused because he had undertaken to drink the cup of suffering to the dregs. He entered the darkness of the victims without illusions in order to share the fate of the others who were hidden in that darkness.

Like them Jesus was a victim of suffering, and if he also triumphed over it he did so by love. Suffering did not turn Jesus in on himself. It did not, as suffering so often does, deprive him of the spiritual strength to be concerned about others. Quite the opposite: Jesus' loving concern reaches all the people around him even as he hangs dying. It reaches his fellow victims on the crosses beside him; it reaches his mother in her grief; it reaches even his executioners, for whom he prays forgiveness. Is this what Simon of Cyrene noticed? Was it as he observed this loving concern of Jesus for others that he began to sense that this crucifixion victim, even in his abject identity with the other victims, was different? Feeling, as Simon must have felt acutely at that moment, the brutality of Roman power, he surely began to see in Jesus neither just one more victim of Rome nor one more brave hero of the Jewish resistance but one who brought the love of God to the tortured and even to the torturers.

Jesus went willingly to his death, but we should not imagine his death as a kind of suicide. Suicide usually is an individual's personal means of escape. The Roman writer Seneca recommended suicide as infinitely preferable to crucifixion. Jesus' cross was precisely not an individual way of death but rather a journey into the deepest solidarity with others. What Jesus accepted willingly was an injustice perpetrated on him by others. As an innocent victim he identified himself with all other innocent victims. Branded a criminal, he identified with all who are condemned, justly or unjustly. Left to suffer and die, he identified with all the victims of human history. For suffering is not just a fact of life for which no one is responsible, though some of it is. Suffering is often the price some people pay for the self-interest, the greed, the neglect of others. This man Jesus, who suffered out of love and loved in his suffering, is the loving solidarity of God with all who suffer.

Following Jesus' way to the cross must involve for us the bringing to remembrance of those with whom Jesus suffered, the victims with whom he identified, especially those who are so easily forgotten, locked away in the prisons of the world, hidden by political propaganda, neglected in the dark places of our world, shut away in their homes where so often the housebound are unvisited, or imprisoned in the frighteningly private griefs and traumas that isolate the afflicted. There are many kinds of forgotten and neglected suffering.

To remember the victims we must take the way of the cross, with Jesus, beyond illusions into the brutal reality of this world. This is a costly and difficult task, but like Simon of Cyrene we shall find it draws us closer to Jesus.

For Prayer & Reflection

With Simon of Cyrene,
pressed by Roman brutality,
witness of Roman oppression,
we recognize the unjust structures of our world:
the tyranny of the powerful over the weak,
the exploitation of the poor by the affluent,
the domination of greed
and the destruction of the earth.

And we recognize you,
Lord Jesus,
as a victim among the victims,
but also more:
as the one who chose the fate of the victimized.

In the brutality of your death
we see the love
that will heal the world.

Help us to see the world
from your place among the victims.
Enable us, with Simon,
to take our share in carrying
your cross, which is also their cross.

Sharing Christ's Cross in Santiago

It was here in Chacabuco that I began to work with the marginal people of Chile and as the weeks passed I grew to love them. Drunk they may have been, alcoholics, rogues and prostitutes they certainly were, but they were a warm people who asked little and accepted gratefully what we could do for them. Most of them were birds of passage, quickly examined, comforted if time and strength allowed, which was not always, and sent on their way with an injection or a prescription or a paper for one of the specialist departments of the teaching hospital next door. Some of them, however, came back to have their stitches out or a particularly complicated wound dressed and these became firm friends. A few of them brought me gifts, the more moving because they were so poor. Occasionally I became personally involved with them and was made desperate by the enormity of their problems and my inability to solve them.

Juanita was a girl of 22 who turned up every few weeks after having had an epileptic fit. One Sunday morning after I had ordered an injection for her the woman with her said, 'She hasn't eaten for four days.' I looked at her more carefully and, finding her pale and thin, asked her if this was so. It was. It was Sunday and there were no social services available and as she could hardly stand I admitted her to the ward. As I interrogated her I learned the full tragedy of her story. Hers was not a congenital epilepsy but had come on after she had fallen head first into an empty swimming pool where she had worked as an instructress. She had fractured her skull and broken her neck and had spent many months in hospital and a few month after her discharge had developed severe and frequent fits. A year ago her mother had died and her father went off to live with another woman leaving Juanita to care as best she could for six little brothers and sisters. I tried hard to help her by arranging appointments with the social worker, but she was unable to get the children into care nor was she able to get any kind of compensation from the owner of the swimming pool. The last time I saw her she turned up just before I was due to go off duty and I managed to get her admitted to the neurological hospital where they tried to control her epilepsy better, but there is no happy ending to her story.

Another case which made me desperate was a young woman of 33 who was in the terminal phase of uterine cancer and who had been firmly told by the radium institute that they could do no more to help her. After she had come for the third time for pain-killing injections I wrote a beseeching letter to the gynecological department of the San Juan de Dios Hospital, our neighbour, and they admitted her to die. She came from the parish where one of my American friends worked and she visited her in hospital and was able to give her some comfort in the last weeks of her life. Many of my patients were sad people and their lives were hard.

As I spent more time in prayer and tried to translate my growing love of God into concrete terms I sought Him more and more in my patients, mindful of Matthew 25: 'I was sick and you visited me.' I tried hard to be more caring and more gentle and much of the time it worked, though when I was tired or hungry or harassed my good intentions and humour left me and I was impatient and unfriendly.

For me, the vision of Christ in man was not one that just happened, it was one that I looked for and found only from time to time. Long hours of praying on my mountain top brought me to a growing consciousness of God in his creation.

> The world is charged with the grandeur of God
> It will flame out like shining from shook foil.
> > G. M. Hopkins, *God's Grandeur*

It was easy to see the image of God in the sun setting behind the Andes or behind the restless tossing of the sea, but the image of Christ in his creatures is a very tarnished one and it is too easy to miss it.

Where is He today?
He is black
and beaten
to a pulp on a Mississippi street.
He falls off a toilet seat
dead
with needle marks in His arms
He stands on a corner, wine soaked.
He is admitted as an OW
into a maternity ward in a city hospital.
He is twenty people living in one tenement room.
He is ten persons living in an Appalachian shack.
He is all this and
more.

Christopher William Jones, *Listen Pilgrim*

As the weeks turned into months and I persevered with my search and
extended my hours of prayer to include the bus journey to work and
odd moments when I wasn't busy I found that my patience was
rewarded and I came to see Him more and more in the broken ones
of Santiago.

Sheila Cassidy

8

MARY MAGDALENE:

ENDURING THE DARKNESS

Reading: Mark 15:33–41

During his ministry Jesus had two kinds of disciples. There were those who traveled with Jesus as he went from place to place, preaching and healing, and who eventually accompanied him to Jerusalem on this last, fateful visit to the capital. These were followers of Jesus in the literal sense. Also there were disciples who stayed in their homes, like the family in Bethany, Mary and Martha and Lazarus. They did not travel with Jesus, but they welcomed Jesus into their homes when he visited their neighborhood.

In the first category, disciples who traveled with Jesus, most readers of the Gospels think most readily of the twelve disciples whom Jesus chose as a group corresponding to the symbolic number of the tribes of Israel. These twelve disciples, of course, were men. But, as well as the Twelve and other male disciples, there were many women disciples of Jesus who traveled around Palestine in Jesus' company and who came to Jerusalem with him on his final visit. We know the names of just seven of them. It is worth rehearsing those names because they get remembered so much less often than the twelve men are: Jesus' mother, Mary; Jesus' aunt, another Mary, the wife of Joseph's brother Clopas; Joanna, a wealthy, aristocratic woman, the wife of Herod's estate manager; Susanna; Salome; Mary the mother of James and Joses; and Mary Magdalene. About some of these women disciples we know very little, just as we know next to nothing about many of the Twelve. We do know that all of these women were present with Jesus at the cross, whereas none of the Twelve were. So to stand with Jesus at the cross, we need to stand there with these women disciples.

Apart from Jesus' mother, the woman we know most about among this group of disciples is Mary Magdalene. We do not know as much about Mary Magdalene as many people think. The one thing many people think they know about Mary Magdalene – that she was a prostitute – is not a fact. The Gospels say nothing of the sort about her. But we know enough about Mary Magdalene to attempt to see Jesus on the cross through her eyes.

Like most of the disciples who traveled with Jesus, Mary came from Galilee. She was from the small village of Migdal or Magdala. She was one of those people the Gospels call *demon-possessed*. This does not mean they were great sinners but that they suffered from evil forces that took over their lives and inflicted all kinds of psychological harm on them. The demon-possessed were not wicked but afflicted by evil. Jesus did not forgive them; he delivered them. Mary of Magdala, the Gospels tell us, was possessed by seven demons until Jesus drove the demons out of her. The number seven indicates that the power of evil over her was total. She had lost all self-possession.

To those who had known her as herself, she was so out of her mind that there seemed nothing of Mary herself left. Something else had taken over. The voice was unrecognizable, and something alien and evil stared out of her mad eyes. Sometimes it was violent and had to be restrained. Sometimes its power was such that Mary would have injured herself badly had she not been restrained.

Jesus delivered her, restored her to herself, and Mary of Magdala became one of Jesus' most devoted disciples. What must it have been like for Mary to be a disciple of Jesus? When the demons left her, it was like walking free from a prison cell in which she had lived in total and perpetual darkness. Jesus led her out into the light of a wholly unexpected dawn in which all was unbelievably new and God's grace and goodness were everywhere to be seen. Mary followed Jesus expecting her own dawn to become the great light of God dawning on the darkness of the whole creation. Many, many others, wherever they went, were being delivered from demons, healed of diseases and disabilities, rescued from sin and death. Everywhere Jesus and his disciples went the darkness was retreating and the light dawning. The devil's great prison house was broken open, and the prisoners were streaming out to freedom. The devil's violence was defeated by Jesus' loving and powerful command. God's kingdom was arriving.

What must it be like for Mary as she stands close to the cross? The darkness has returned. A preternatural gloom shrouds Golgotha at noon. But the outward darkness is simply the symbol of the spiritual darkness Mary's spirit enters on Golgotha. All she had lived for has come to this. The one she had lived for is lost to her, and all the hopes she put in him have been destroyed. He who had defeated evil in her life is now defeated by evil. He who had freed her from the violence she suffered now suffers violence himself. The dawn has proved a false dawn; the darkness is returning to envelop creation as it always had.

The darkness Mary Magdalene enters on Golgotha is not, of course, simply a return to the isolated darkness of her demonic prison. Now she enters not her own but Jesus' darkness. And Jesus' darkness is the darkness of the whole world whose hope, she had thought, lay in him. This is the desolation of vast hopes raised and defeated. For Mary there is no light ahead for her or for the world, nothing but the bleakness and the blackness that surround her on Golgotha. The light of the world goes out as she watches Jesus die in agony and hears his enemies taunt: 'He saved others, but he cannot save himself.' Since he cannot save himself, he can no longer save others. The light goes out and the darkness returns to the world.

But to stand with Mary Magdalene at the cross we must not only imagine her desolation. We must also realize that Mary remains to the end a faithful disciple of Jesus. She *endures* the darkness and the desolation. Powerless to help, she nevertheless stays. She watches what is unbearable to watch. It is Mary's faithfulness that brings her to this place of desolation and keeps her there through the three hours of darkness to the end. She remains in the darkness. She endures the loss of all hope. She knows there can be no consolation. She remains with Jesus to no purpose other than the faithfulness of her love for Jesus. And because she stays, endures the darkness, follows the dead body to the grave, returns to the tomb to experience yet another stage of desolation when she finds the body itself has been taken from her, because she remains faithful through the darkness, without consolation, Mary of Magdala is still there on Easter morning, the first to meet the risen Christ in the bright dawn of his resurrection.

Mary had not been wrong about the dawning of the light of God on all creation. She had not been wrong to find in her own liberation the great hope for liberation of all people and all things from evil. But to bring light and liberation to all Jesus had to enter the darkness himself. And so Mary's desolation was not mistaken either. The darkness, the violence, the subjection to evil were real. Jesus himself endured them without consolation. God his Father abandoned him to death. 'My God, my God, why have you forsaken me?' he cried.

The darkness of Golgotha imaged Jesus' own desolation, and it was his darkness Mary truly entered and endured. Faithfulness without light, without hope or consolation, was exactly what was demanded of her. She endured with Jesus the very blackest hours of world history, and conversely he, dying and desolate, endured them with her.

Only so could the light of resurrection dawn on the whole creation. This is the mystery of salvation: that Jesus did not abolish the darkness with a word of command or the wave of a wand of divine power. He entered it. He reached the lowest depths where the most desolate of the world lie helpless. He entered, among other depths, that prison of the seven demons in which Mary herself had languished. He lay among the charred bodies of the babies burned alive in Auschwitz. He shared the numbed horror of their parents beyond consolation. He sat in the isolated darkness of the condemned cell, physical or mental, and he felt the collective darkness of Bosnia and Rwanda, the darkness that thickens as more and more succumb to its power. Jesus plumbed the depths of darkness because only so could he bring with him all he found there into the dawn of the new creation of the world. He died the death of the most abandoned, so that even the most abandoned might share his resurrection.

But Mary Magdalene does not know this. She simply endures the darkness, faithful to Jesus even in desolation.

If such a place of darkness is not one in which most of us find ourselves often, we all know people who are there or have been there. We know people who find themselves there all too often. We know about people who live their whole lives in the shadows of such a place. But all of us glimpse it in our own experience from time to time. Sometimes it may be only for a short period, in some black mood of hopelessness about our lives, when everything seems without meaning, or of despair over the evil of the world, when belief in God seems suddenly impossible. Those may be fleeting but serious glimpses of the desolation of Calvary. Or there may be longer experiences, such as in bereavement, when there seems only a sort of daily bleakness to be got through, and no hope beyond it seems real. These experiences can be outward experiences: bereavement or loss, isolation or loneliness, rejection or pain. They can be purely inward experiences: depression or despair or, worst of all, loss of the sense of God. In these experiences too the darkness seems to hang over us and to press down upon us and to cut off any sight of a future worth living for.

There are two ways in which such experiences of darkness can relate to Jesus on the cross in the darkness of Golgotha. In the first, we find Jesus Christ with us in our darkness. On the cross he shared our darkness. His loving presence with us in our darkness lightens it. In our desolation we find the comfort of his presence. Because he suffered even abandonment by God, he is God's very presence with us even in abandonment. It is like being visited in the condemned cell by someone who loves us enough to come and share the experience with us. Bringing God's love into our darkness, Jesus removes the lovelessness at the heart of our darkness. Or when we look out at the darkness of our world, the seeming absence of God in such killing fields as Rwanda or the desolating darkness of ignorance of God and hatred of God that clouds so much of our own society, still we can recognize God's presence in it because we recognize God in the darkness of Golgotha.

That is the first kind of experience of the cross in our darkness: when Jesus' presence with us in it brings God's love into our lovelessness and God's presence into our forsakenness. But there is also a second kind of experience of the cross which is closer to Mary Magdalene's. Sometimes in our own darkness or in that of the world we can find only the darkness that Jesus endured. We feel without God, and we continue to do so. We find no hope or consolation. We simply find ourselves there in the darkness with Jesus in his desolation. Like Mary, all we can do is stay in the darkness, waiting, not knowing there is anything to wait for. Mary's love and faithfulness are all that keep her there. Because of her love and faithfulness she has nowhere else to go. Out of such experiences, for us as for Mary, come fresh experiences of God. But they cannot seem like that. At the time, for us as for Mary, there is only the darkness, only the faithful staying there, hanging on, until, with the surprise of Mary in the garden by the empty tomb, we hear behind us, at first perhaps without recognition, the voice of the risen Christ calling us by name.

For Prayer & Reflection

God the Father of our Lord Jesus,
we remember those for whom,
like Mary Magdalene,
there is darkness at noon
and inconsolable loss.

We pray for those
who in their faithfulness to Jesus
endure his desolation.
Be with them in the darkness
until the light of your presence dawns for them again.

We pray for those
who in their desolation
have not yet known Jesus –
that in his desolation
they may find your presence
with them in theirs.

In the plight of a world
that lacks your love
and in the tragedy of a world
that refuses your presence,

help us to see Jesus crucified
as your presence in the world's darkness.
Help us to find in him
your unfailing love for your world,
his faith in your purpose for your world,
our hope for the noontime sunshine
of your presence in your whole creation.

We pray for ourselves
when the shadow of death falls on our lives
or the prison doors shut us in.
Lord Jesus,
let us neither lose sight of you on Calvary
nor fail to meet you again in the garden.

God in the Darkness
Following the sudden death of the writer's son at the age of twenty-five

I am at an impasse, and you, O God, have brought me here. From my
earliest days, I heard of you. From my earliest days, I believed in you.
I shared in the life of your people: in their prayers, in their work, in
their songs, in their listening for your speech and in their watching
for your presence. For me your yoke was easy. On me your presence
smiled.

Noon has darkened. As fast as she could say, 'He's dead', the light
dimmed. And where are you in this darkness? I learned to spy you in
the light. Here in this darkness I cannot find you. If I had never
looked for you, or looked but never found, I would not feel this pain
of your absence. Or is it not your absence in which I dwell but your
elusive troubling presence?

Will my eyes adjust to this darkness? Will I find you in the dark –

not in the streaks of light which remain, but in the darkness? Has anyone ever found you there? Did they love what they saw? Did they see love? And are there songs for singing when the light has gone dim? The songs I learned were all of praise and thanksgiving and repentance. Or in the dark, is it best to wait in silence?

Nicholas Wolterstorff

Three Hours of Darkness
It was the sixth hour, and a great darkness spread over all the land.

Why did it grow dark at this point? What had happened between heaven and earth? The scene was still the same, no one had thought up any new torture, the soldiers were still throwing dice for his tunic: the passion was stagnating in funereal expectation. But what was really happening was a death inside a death. During those three hours, until the ninth, he was wrestling with an even worse executioner, he was undergoing a more appalling annihilation. As in the garden, there was again this monstrous silence: but here it was a thousand times worse, because suddenly everything – his goodness and men's malice, the gentle cornfields and the polecats that laid them waste – all seemed utterly and grotesquely pointless.

As from the sixth hour the dying Christ was an orphan. He no longer had his mother, he'd given her to someone else. And now the Father died on him; those three hours of darkness were the agony of the Father in his brain.

'My God, why have you abandoned me?'

The other words that he said from the cross were forced out in a weak voice from an exhausted body. But these he shouted *with a great voice*; it was a shout which had to reach the most desperate and remote, those who would remain unmoved by the groans and the blood; all those who, when going over the story of the passion heard from a priest in their childhood, say: 'But my life is far worse than that afternoon on the cross.'

Within the layers of that darkness he was the God of those people. Where's the tragic pit in the depths of which man is most sad and most stifled by a deadly sickness? It's here: Christ plunged into it and was equal with all the unhappy people who have lost the Father; because he never reckoned to be born and to die among the living without sharing the ninth hour with us all.

Luigi Santucci

9

THE CENTURION AT THE FOOT OF THE CROSS:

AN ACCIDENTAL WITNESS

Reading: Mark 15:33–39

'Surely this man was the Son of God.' What exactly was it, we might wonder, that this campaign-hardened professional soldier saw that evoked this surprising confession? We shall never know precisely what he meant by his words, but they constitute an unexpected verdict on Jesus in the degradation of his suffering and death.

Let us begin by thinking for a moment about this man. He would have been around the then known world, seen many things, no doubt fought in many battles. He would have been familiar with death and all that accompanied it. But now, having reached the rank of centurion, he found himself in one of the farthest-flung corners of the empire, with a less than glorious assignment as commander of Pilate's execution squad. Day by day he carried out the orders handed down to him, dispensing in the most barbarous way with the criminal scum of Palestine. Perhaps as he came home from another day's killing to his wife and children he could forget the unpleasantness, the cries of the dying, the contempt of the crowds for victim and executioner alike. And perhaps he couldn't. But his sensitivities, if he had any left, would have been dulled long since to human death and dying. One death on Golgotha would be much like any other, no matter how many fascinating variations on a theme his men managed to conjure up for their amusement out of the basic pattern of crucifixion.

Today, as he marched his men out again to that godforsaken hill, as they herded the prisoners like so many cattle to the slaughter, this man would supervise the crucifixion of Jesus from Nazareth. And suddenly, out of the blue, he found himself affected by this death. He had seen it all before. Yet something about this man in his death made so deep an impression on him that it called forth, demanded even, this almost involuntary statement: 'Surely this man was the Son of God'. Was it a statement, or was it a question? Was it a carefully judged verdict, or was it blurted out without any serious thought for those who would hear? Certainly it wasn't the sort of thing that the average rank-and-file soldier expects to hear from his sergeant major!

And the words are charged with irony. From a human point of view we might reach several conclusions about this pathetic figure on just one more cross among the many that littered the roadsides of Palestine, tributes to the ruthless efficiency of Roman justice and a gradually falling crime rate. But few things can be more remote from this set of circumstances on most accounts of the matter than the thought that here we see one loved and blessed by God. The suggestion beggars belief. Surely God would never allow one whom he loved to come to such an awful end? It's not surprising that the Jews entertained the view that one who hung on a tree was accursed by God: abandoned by him and beyond hope or salvation. To be crucified was for anyone who had had anything like a decent Sunday-school education in Jesus' day a clear sign of having been rejected by God.

And those terrible words from the cross, spoken by the dying Jesus, seem at first to confirm this, not to contradict it. 'My God, my God, why have you forsaken me?' As we have seen, the darkness of the cross for Jesus lay not just in its physical torment and trauma, not just in the inevitability of death, but in the utter separation from and abandonment by God of which it was so potent a symbol. How ironic that in this context and hearing these words from Jesus' lips anyone should presume to conclude that this man was in truth God's own beloved Son, the one in whom here supremely God was well pleased, the object of God's constant love and care and blessing.

The Gospels let us into the secret early on that this is so. They portray Jesus as one whose life was one long conversation in prayer with his Father. It was his constant joy and delight to do his Father's will and work. Mark's Gospel opens with a voice from heaven at Jesus' baptism that leaves us in no doubt about God's verdict on Jesus, a voice that the centurion's confession at the Gospel's end clearly echoes and confirms, forming a set of theological bookends to the writer's evaluation of Jesus. How awful then for Jesus to experience the pain of being separated for the first time from the Father whom he loved. Maybe it was the evident sincerity and pain poured out in those words from the cross that broke through the callus built up by years of exposure to death and degradation and pierced the heart and spirit of the centurion. On this cross was a man who loved God, for only one who genuinely loves much can be hurt this much by separation.

The cry of Jesus from the cross can be likened to the cry of a small child accidentally separated from its parents in a seething crowd. It is the cry of a love that finds itself apparently faced with loss of the reciprocal love that it knows from moment to moment, the love that grants it its identity and upon which it depends for its being and its world. When the experience of this love appears to be lost even for a moment the child cries out in fear and pain. For Jesus to experience separation from his Father was the most awful thing that could happen to him, by comparison with which the pain of the nails and the scourging was as nothing.

The centurion's judgment, that this pathetic, exhausted, bedraggled, abused, sad-looking victim of the ultimate human injustice was and is God's own Son, may not be a likely conclusion; but it is the conclusion that Christian faith is driven to in spite of all the appearances. And it is a conclusion that forces us to reconsider the ways in which we habitually think of God, the images that spring readily and uninvited to mind when we use the word or hear it used, the accouterments that we assume to attach to the office of God. They are, as Studdert Kennedy's poem 'High and Lifted Up' reminds us, all too often images of an untrammeled power and glory and majesty and splendor, the sort of power that we associate with human lords and overlords. It is a power that seems to leave little space for vulnerability or pain or weakness or divine pathos.

Yet the centurion's words contain the seeds of a perception that tears such a picture of God wide open, a perception that goes beyond anything he can have intended but that pushes its logic to the most radical and unexpected conclusion. God and crucifixion, God and suffering, God and humiliation, God and grief and pain, God and tragedy; these are not exclusive opposites. The man who dies on the cross can be God's own Son, because God is not incapable of or unwilling to be involved with such experiences. The most radical conclusion is reached only when the cross is viewed (as it has to be) in the light of the perception that Jesus is none other than God in our midst, Immanuel, the great I AM. For then what we must say is not that what it means to be God is big enough to incorporate the darkness of Golgotha, but that Golgotha itself, in all its terrible darkness, shows us more of what is characteristic of God and his love than any-thing else ever could, that God is revealed most fully in the pain and vulnerability of Jesus' death.

Many sermons and books have been written in an attempt to explain what happens upon the cross. But in a sense the impact of the story lies in its telling rather than in analyzing and explaining. As we stand with the centurion and watch what goes on, either we find our-selves drawn in and moved by it or we don't. Either we discover ourselves to be mysteriously bound up with what is happening and somehow know that what happens happens in some sense 'for us' or we don't. Either we are moved to cast ourselves down before the cross of this man Jesus in thankful praise, or we are left cold, watching with only a detached fascination as he opens his arms and prepares to embrace the awfulness of death and hell.

For Prayer & Reflection

High and Lifted Up

Seated on the throne of power with the sceptre in Thine hand,
While a host of eager angels ready for Thy Service stand.
So it was the prophet saw Thee, in his agony of prayer,
While the sound of many waters swelled in music on the air,
Swelled until it burst like thunder in a shout of perfect praise,
'Holy, Holy, Holy Father, Potentate of years and days.
Thine the Kingdom, Thine the glory, Thine the splendour of the sun,
Thine the wisdom, Thine the honour, Thine the crown of victory won.'

So it was the prophet saw Thee, so this artist saw Thee too,
Flung his vision into colour, mystery of gold and blue.
But I stand in woe and wonder; God, my God, I cannot see,
Darkness deep and deeper darkness – all the world is dark to me.

Where is power? Where is glory? Where is any victory won?
Where is wisdom? Where is honour? Where the splendour of the
sun?

God, I hate this splendid vision — all its splendour is a lie,
Splendid fools see splendid folly, splendid mirage born to die.
As imaginary waters to an agony of thirst,
As the vision of a banquet to a body hunger-cursed,
As the thought of anaesthetic to a soldier mad with pain,
While his torn and tortured body turns and twists and writhes again,
So this splendid lying vision turns within my doubting heart,
Like a bit of rusty bayonet in a torn and festering part.

Preachers give it me for comfort, and I curse them to their face,
Puny, petty-minded priestlings prate to me of power and grace;
Prate of power and boundless wisdom that takes count of little birds,
Sentimental poisoned sugar in a sickening stream of words.
Platitudinously pious far beyond all doubts and fears,
They will patter of God's mercy that can wipe away our tears.
All their speech is drowned in sobbing, and I hear the great world
groan,
As I see a million mothers sitting weeping all alone,
See a host of English maidens making pictures in the fire,
While a host of broken bodies quiver still on German wire.

And I hate the God of Power on His hellish heavenly throne,
Looking down on rape and murder, hearing little children moan.
Though a million angels hail Thee King of Kings, yet cannot I.
There is nought can break the silence of my sorrow save the cry,
'Thou who rul'st this world of sinners with Thy heavy iron rod,
Was there ever any sinner who has sinned the sin of God?
Was there ever any dastard who would stand and watch a Hun
Ram his bayonet through the bowels of a baby just for fun?

Praise to God in Heaven's highest and in all the depths be praise,
Who in all His works is brutal, like a beast in all his ways.'

God, the God I love and worship, reigns in sorrow on the Tree,
Broken, bleeding, but unconquered, very God of God to me.

All that showy pomp of splendour, all that sheen of angel wings,
Was but borrowed from the baubles that surround our earthly kings.
Thought is weak and speech is weaker, and the vision that He sees
Strikes with dumbness any preacher, brings him humbly to his knees.
But the word that Thou has spoken borrows nought from kings and
thrones,
Vain to rack a royal palace for the echo of Thy tones.
In a manger, in a cottage, in an honest workman's shed,
In the homes of humble peasants, and the simple lives they led,
In the life of one an outcast and a vagabond on earth,
In the common things He valued, and proclaimed of priceless worth,
And above all in the horror of the cruel death He died,
Thou has bid us seek Thy glory, in a criminal crucified.
And we find it – for Thy glory is the glory of Love's loss,
And Thou hast no other splendour but the splendour of the Cross.
For in Christ I see the martyrs and the beauty of their pain,
And in Him I hear the promise that my dead shall rise again.

High and lifted up, I see Him on the eternal Calvary,
And two piercèd hands are stretching east and west o'er land and sea.
On my knees I fall and worship that great Cross that shines above,
For the very God of Heaven is not Power, but Power of Love.

G. A. Studdert Kennedy

A Prayer

Lord Jesus,
as we behold your solidarity with
the victims of injustice,
the degraded,
the despised,
the suffering
and the dying,
may we discover hope in knowing your presence
with us in our own darkness
and strength to follow you
in sharing and bearing the darkness of others.

Amen.

10

NICODEMUS:

SEEING THE KINGDOM OF GOD

Readings: John 3:1–10; 19:19–22, 38–42

Crucifixion was meant to be a deterrent. The horror of crucifixion, the public shame and the agony, was supposed to deter anyone else who witnessed it from committing the same crime as the crucified person had committed. So the Romans often pinned on a cross a statement of the crime for which the person had been condemned. The crime had to be publicly known if others were to be deterred from such crime. This is what Pilate did in Jesus' case. Jesus' crime was that he claimed to be a king. He had confessed as much in Pilate's examination of him. True, Pilate was not inclined to take the matter very seriously. He did not think Jesus was really a political threat to

Roman rule in Palestine, and he was inclined to let Jesus go. But the Jewish chief priests for once had the upper hand. Surely, they pointed out, anyone who claimed to be a king was ipso facto an enemy of the Roman emperor. Pilate simply could not afford to be seen to condone someone calling himself king of the Jews. So the chief priests, wily politicians that they were, got their way against the Roman governor's better judgment. Not that Pilate, cynical politician that he was, cared about the issue itself. But he hated being outmaneuvered by the Jewish authorities.

So Jesus died with the inscription – in three languages so that any literate person could read it – pinned above his head. The chief priests wanted it worded more carefully. They wanted Pilate to make it clear that this was only the claim Jesus made. He was not, of course, really the king of the Jews. But Pilate was getting his own back by having his little joke against the Jewish authorities and the Jewish nation he despised. *This* is their king! This is the sort of king they deserve – this crucified man, this pathetic failure! So Pilate insisted the wording must stand. In one of the great ironies of providence, Roman judicial custom and the petty political tensions in the government of Judaea conspired to produce this result: Jesus died with an inscription proclaiming that he was the king of Israel. The inscription was written not only in Hebrew, as befitted the king of Israel, but also in Greek, the international language of the day, so that everyone could understand it, and also in Latin, the language of the power that ruled the world.

Jesus' claim to kingship was a claim not only to rule over Israel but also to universal rule, and a claim therefore that challenged the universal rule of Rome. In other words, Jesus was the Messiah, who was God's anointed king of his people Israel, but also, as Israel fully expected, the king over all people, who would implement God's rule over all the world, whose rule was truly divine and therefore opposed to the divine pretensions of Rome. Rejected by the Jewish leaders, crucified by Rome, Jesus had apparently failed to be this messianic king. But at very the point which to Pilate and the chief priests made his failure laughably obvious, Jesus was, as it were, proclaimed to the world as its king. Could anyone, seeing Jesus die, take that claim seriously? Could anyone at that moment regard him as truly the king of the Jews, truly the ruler of all? We might well think it unlikely. But could any politician, anyone who moved in those ruling circles in which Pilate and the chief priests conversed, collaborated, intrigued and, like politicians the world over, hated each other while depending on each other – could anyone in that world of very worldly politics have continued to take seriously Jesus' claim to be king when they saw him crucified and dead? Surely not.

Yet it was precisely someone who moved in those circles who did. When Pilate gave Joseph of Arimathea permission to take Jesus' body for burial, a man called Nicodemus also took a hand in the events. It was Nicodemus who ensured that Jesus' burial was a burial fit for a king. Nicodemus came with half a hundredweight of extremely expensive spices. A vast expense, and a vast quantity. We should not imagine Nicodemus sneaking out there, hoping to do this without anyone noticing. He would have a whole procession of servants carrying the spices. Nicodemus's action was an act of conspicuous honor to a man condemned and executed for treason against Roman rule. But in the cultural code of the day, someone worth half a hundredweight of spices for his burial would have to be a king at least. Nicodemus was saying, very publicly and so very courageously, that the inscription on the cross was true. Jesus was king. And even if a dead king would not, while he stayed dead, worry either Romans or chief priests too much, Nicodemus was exposing himself dangerously by treating this man as indeed a king.

For Nicodemus was an important person. Most of Jesus' disciples we have met in this book were people of no social standing, no power or influence. But Nicodemus is quite different. With Nicodemus we move in exalted social circles. He is a wealthy aristocrat, a member of one of the great families of Jerusalem. Members of his family got into the records of Jewish history for their prominent political roles. They were remembered in Jewish tradition for their fabulous wealth and their patronage of the Pharisees. They had a palatial mansion in Jerusalem, a winter residence down in the warmer climate of Jericho and vast estates out in the country. They were one of the great families who formed the little ruling clique of Jewish aristocrats, who under the general surveillance of Rome ran most of the affairs of Judaea. Nicodemus's family were not quite at the center of power, because they were Pharisees, not Sadducees. The chief priests and most of the ruling aristocrats were Sadducees, but Nicodemus was one of those few Pharisees who, just because they belonged to wealthy families too important to be left out, moved in the circles of power, forming a sort of minority group in uneasy coalition with the Sadducean chief priests. Not quite at the center of power, but close to it, Nicodemus was certainly a man of power and influence. He was a man whose natural interests aligned him with the Jewish leaders who saw Jesus as a political threat.

Nicodemus was a wealthy aristocrat, but he was also a Pharisee of Pharisees, a learned rabbi. That was the capacity in which he first encountered Jesus. When Jesus was first in Jerusalem, Nicodemus with a group of his disciples came to Jesus one evening for a serious religious discussion with Jesus and his disciples. He came as one rabbi visiting another, but already he saw a little more than that in Jesus, and already the political issue arose. We should not imagine that any first-century Jew, or any first-century Roman or any first-century anybody, could keep religion and politics apart. When Jesus, in his very first words to Nicodemus, referred to the kingdom of God, he was raising the Jewish political issue, the issue of God's rule over God's people and his world and the question of what this meant in practical political terms when in practice it was Rome that ruled, claiming divinity and usurping the rule of Israel's God. Whenever Jesus mentioned the kingdom of God, this would occur to his hearers, but here, on the only occasion we see Jesus in friendly conversation with a member of the ruling Jewish elite, there is a special resonance. Nicodemus belonged to the group who ruled because Rome let them rule, who supported Rome in return for Rome's support for their own power. In the eyes of many more radical Jews, they were the betrayers of the national cause and of Israel's God.

This political issue – at the heart of Jewish religious concerns – concerned Nicodemus, we can be sure. Nicodemus was a sincere man. Unlike the chief priests, he was not using religion for his own self-interested political ends. Though he was a member of the ruling elite, entrammeled in the power structure that cooperated with Roman rule, Nicodemus was not really happy with that role. He was looking for a radical alternative to the cynical and self-interested politics he knew so well in the traffic between the high priest's council chamber and the governor's residence. Those power politics of which we see a good example in the process that led to Jesus' death Nicodemus already disliked. He was looking for the kingdom of God, for something more like the rule of the God of Israel described in the Hebrew Scriptures he studied daily. When Nicodemus finally honored the crucified and dead man Jesus as God's true king he showed that he had recognized this radical alternative in Jesus.

Just how radical an alternative it was Nicodemus could begin to see from Jesus' first words to him, puzzling and problematic as he found them. 'No one can see the kingdom of God without being born from above,' Jesus says rather abruptly, taking Nicodemus straight to the heart of the issue. 'No one can see the kingdom of God without being born from above (or born again)': we should remember that Nicodemus was not only a born Jew, but also a born aristocrat. He owed his place among the Jewish ruling authorities to his *birth*. But that, Jesus says, counts for nothing in the kingdom of God. Jesus' radical alternative to the power politics Nicodemus knew so well is not some reshuffling of the same political pack. It is so different it requires new birth to participate in it. New birth is also birth from above, because the kingdom of God comes from God above.

As Jesus said later in his dramatic confrontation with the local representative of Roman rule, 'My kingdom is not from this world. If my kingdom were from this world, my followers would be fighting to keep me from being handed over to the Jewish authorities.' Jesus' rule is not from this world, because it is from above, from God. He does not mean that it exists in some purely otherworldly sphere that has no relation to worldly politics. This is not a safely spiritual alternative that leaves the politics of Pilate and Caiaphas intact and untroubled. That's where Pilate makes a big mistake, because Pilate can only think of politics in his cynical Roman way in which military might is all that counts.

In a world where might is divine right, Jesus' claim that his rule cannot be furthered by military force makes him a harmless fool. What kind of rule can there be that doesn't depend on military force? But we miss the radical force of Jesus' words, in effect we make Pilate's mistake, if we say: This can be only an otherworldly, purely spiritual, purely religious, wholly nonpolitical kind of rule. Jesus does not say his kingdom is not in this world. He says it is not *from* this world. It does not derive its values or its methods from the same kind of sources as Pilate's rule does. Its values and its methods are radically different because they come from God. This is God's rule which radically challenges and impacts upon Rome's rule precisely because it *does not* play the same game in the same way. It is not innocuous to Rome or to the chief priests, to the power politics Nicodemus knows so well. It is far more of a threat to them than Barabbas and the Jewish militant revolutionaries are, because it challenges their values and their methods so much more radically.

We do not know how far Nicodemus got in seeing this before the crucifixion. But it must have been the way in which Jesus was condemned to die that finally convinced him that Jesus really did represent God's rule. Because Nicodemus belonged to the political elite and moved in the circles of power in Jerusalem, he, perhaps sooner than any of the other disciples, was able to recognize Jesus as

God's radical alternative to the way God's people and God's world were being ruled by the likes of Pilate and Caiaphas. What did Nicodemus see as Jesus was condemned to die? Pilate's cynical *realpolitik*. The chief priests' astute self-interest. And the two coming together in a shocking climax to the negotiations. Mockingly Pilate says, 'Shall I crucify your King?' The chief priests reply, 'We have no king but Caesar.'

In their determination to protect their own power by rejecting Jesus, the chief priests endorse Rome's claim to absolute power. In Jewish terms they reject God. To a conscientious rabbi like Nicodemus, 'We have no king but Caesar' is apostasy from the God of Israel. It rejects God's rule in favor of Rome's claim to sole and divine rule. This is what the chief priests' self-serving political compromise has finally come to. Nicodemus can no longer have any part in it. But in that case where can he see God's rule? Where else than in the alternative Pilate and the chief priests conspire to reject? Precisely the man neither Pilate nor the chief priests can recognize as the king of Israel is the one who must truly be the king of Israel. He is the king come from God, as Pilate and the chief priests so evidently do not. He is the king one must be born from above to serve. In the radical alternative God's rule presents to Pilate's and Caiaphas's concepts of rule, this crucified man is the king. His crucifixion means nothing less than the coming of God's kingdom.

So for Pilate and the chief priests the cross refutes Jesus' claim to be king, if refutation were needed. But for Nicodemus it refutes Pilate's and the chief priest's respective claims to represent divine rule. In this radical polarizing of the alternatives, Nicodemus can no longer have any truck with political compromise. He finally burns his boats. He throws in his lot with Jesus. He publicly honors him as king. He steps completely outside the circle that binds the governor's residence and the high priest's council chamber together. He accepts whatever it might mean to find God's rule exemplified, even *implemented* in the humiliated and suffering Jesus. He commits himself to

whatever that might involve by way of reversal of conventional thinking about power and status, about what really matters and what really
gets things done in the real world. He commits himself to whatever it
means to think that neither Pilate nor the chief priests in fact have
the last word as they think they do, that beyond the petty game they
play with each other actually God holds and plays a trump card of
which they have no conception. When Nicodemus saw Jesus crucified
and when he recognized this crucified Jesus as truly the king who
rules for God, then (might we not say?) Nicodemus was truly born
from above, born again of the Spirit of God. For 'no one', Jesus had
said to him, 'can see the kingdom of God without being born from
above.'

For Prayer & Reflection

Lord Jesus, with Nicodemus we recognize you
as the ruler of all
not in spite of your cross
but because of it.
We see your power in your weakness,
your glory in your humiliation,
your sovereignty in your self-giving service,
your victory in your death.

Help us not to be taken in by the illusions of evil,
by the apparent dominance of the forces that oppose God in this
world
by the apparently overwhelming influence
of forces that corrupt life and destroy creation.
Help us to resist them.

Keep us from the temptations of power and influence,
from using them to serve the idols
of self-advancement or the causes we favor,
from treating other people as means to our ends,
from disregarding others on the way to our ends.

Help us to recognize the power of truth and love,
help us to acknowledge you as the only Lord.

Your kingdom come.

The Tempter

He watched from behind some large, black rocks as the man from
Nazareth came once more to his kingdom. He let him pass by, then
slid out from his hiding place and called after him. 'Here I am, Jesus,
behind you!' His voice moved over the face of the wilderness, and
called forth its desolation. 'Have you had second thoughts, that you
come here again? Are you prepared now to accept my propositions,
agree to our little plan?'

He circled slowly round Jesus, looking as if he might pounce at any
moment. 'We could be a great team, you and I. Look at all you have
achieved! And in such a short space of time, too! Few could have
become such a conspicuous failure in such as short time as you have
done! Yet I have been impressed by you. You have great potential,
Jesus. If only you had followed my advice in the first place, things
would not have come to this. But it is not too late.'

His circling began to get faster. 'We could try again, try this time
to impress the right people, try this time to work some miracles out
in the open, in the market place, where people will notice. You have
been working in alleyways, in dark corners. You have taken the blind
and lame off the stage, away from the bright lights, and healed them

in the wings. That won't do. Razzmatazz! Razzmatazz! That's what
we need!'

By now he was dancing a weird, frenetic jig. 'Let me be your direc-
tor, and I will make you a star, Jesus! They might even get to calling
you "Son of God!" You see, it's not *what* you do that's wrong, it's the
way that you do it.'

Suddenly he slowed down, and resumed his measured, sinister
prowl. 'I have heard that you walked on the water and calmed the
storm. But I did not see it. I was there. I always am, aren't I, Jesus?
But I did not see anything. I have many friends living round the Sea
of Galilee, but they saw nothing, heard nothing. Some of them were
out in boats at the time, but did not catch your footfall on the waves,
nor did the storm cease for them. Two of them were drowned. I knew
them well. Why did you not save them, Jesus? Were they the wrong
side of the lake? You have to be the right side of the lake to get saved,
Jesus, is that it? To the devil with the rest, is that it?' He laughed.

'Now, if you and I were in partnership, we could save everybody, no
questions asked. "Salvation for all!" That could be our motto, and
people could have it whether they wanted it or not. After all, salvation is salvation, never mind how you come by it.'

At last he stopped, and stood waiting for an answer.

'You and your friends are so hard of hearing,' said Jesus, 'so blind to
what is around you, so dead to all feeling! Did you sense nothing at
all, as you lay there in the dark turbulence of those waters? Did you
not feel anything as I stepped upon your back, as I touched your wild
chaos with my finger, and raised my hand to give you my blessing? I
suppose you were expecting hobnailed boots. But that is not my way,
Satan. I have a light touch. I do things on the quiet. You do not know
the meaning of gentleness. Yet I had hoped you would feel one foot-
step, and begin to feel my calm. I had wanted your friends to see just
a little beneath the surface, to sense my creation beneath your
destruction. One day they will find it. You do not believe me, Satan,
but my gentleness is stronger than your violence, my humility more

enduring than your arrogance, and my laughter and my love lie too
deep for your bitterness and cynicism.'

'Come, then!' said Satan savagely, and he stepped forward, as if to
take hold of Jesus. 'Come, let me take you to the top of a high mountain, and show you the kingdoms of the world and the glory of them!'

They turned and went up together, till they reached the very summit and the world lay at their feet.

'Look!' shouted Satan against the howl of the wind. 'Look, there
they are! The petty kingdoms of this paltry world! You could have had
them for your own, if only you had been willing to co-operate. But
see, they are mine! Look at them tearing each other apart, dismem-
bering the world! You have heard it said:

"Thou hast made him little less than God,
and dost crown him with glory and honour."

But what I say to you is this:

"I have made him little higher than the demons,
and girded him with lust and greed!"

I have made these precious human beings of yours the most aggres-
sive and destructive of all your creatures. The earthworm and the
orchid may not yet be mine, nor the antelope and the wren, but
humanity at least is mine! You have lost them, Jesus! You have lost,
lost, Jesus!' The hideous dance began again, but Jesus did not wait this
time for it to cease.

'You see only the dark,' Jesus cried. 'You do not see in the dark, you
see only the darkness itself, and you teach others to do the same.'

'And you see only the sunset, the daffodil, and the butterfly!'
shouted Satan as he spat on the rocks.

'If I see only them, then I see more than you do, Satan. But, no. I
see the dark, also.'

'But you do not *know* the dark as I know it. You do not see it for what it is.'

Jesus pointed to scars on his hands and feet. 'Do you not recognise them, Satan? You put them there yourself. Oh, I know your darkness. I have been there, but you were so blind, you did not notice me. Now I have come out of the dark, Satan, into the light, the light that I created, the light that is myself. You had no hold over me in the beginning, and you have none now. I am risen from the dead, Satan, and everywhere there is resurrection! Your days are numbered, and one day this wilderness of yours will become again the garden of God.'

Satan no longer heard him because of the howl of the wind, and he did not see through the mist clinging to his mountain top, as Jesus walked down the mountain side towards those petty kingdoms of this paltry world. He was left a solitary figure on the summit, mesmerised by his own deadly dance, leaping and jerking in unending circles round nothing but himself.

Trevor Dennis

11

THE DISCIPLE JESUS LOVED:

THE WITNESS TO THE TRUTH

Readings: Zechariah 12:10; 13:1;
John 13:21–26; 19:23–27

We began our reflections with a disciple whose gift was her perceptiveness: Mary of Bethany. Her love for Jesus enabled her to intuit Jesus' willing acceptance of his death, enabled her to see that Jesus must die and, alone among the disciples at that point, enabled her to accept his death as he did. We end our reflections with another disciple whose gift was his perceptiveness, a disciple whose special closeness to Jesus enabled him to understand, more perceptively than any of the disciples, the meaning of Jesus' death. Mary, when she anointed Jesus, accepted that Jesus must die but probably could not tell why. The disciple we now meet came, not at once, but through his reflective entering into the reality of the cross which he witnessed, to a profound understanding of its meaning for us all.

We shall call him the disciple Jesus loved or the Beloved Disciple, because his Gospel gives him no name. It refers to him simply as 'the disciple Jesus loved.' He may well have been called John, which was one of the most common Jewish names of the time, and so later Church tradition confused him with that more famous John, the son of Zebedee, the fisherman, one of the most prominent of Jesus' twelve disciples. Church tradition sometimes fused or confused disciples who are quite distinct within the Gospels themselves. The two Marys – Mary of Bethany and Mary Magdalene – were identified and a sort of composite portrait created. We have kept the two Marys distinct in this book, because in the Gospels they are different people. In the same way we should now attend to the Beloved Disciple without muddling him up with John the son of Zebedee. We shall keep him anonymous, as his Gospel itself does. To call him the Beloved Disciple says far more about him than a name would.

'The disciple Jesus loved' – that phrase leads us to expect a figure of key importance in the Gospel story. In fact he is remarkably unobtrusive, slipping in and out of the narrative of John's Gospel, sometimes so as we hardly notice. Probably he is the mysteriously anonymous member of the first pair of disciples, along with Andrew, in the first chapter of the Gospel. He and Andrew, already disciples of John the Baptist, hear their master proclaim Jesus to be the Lamb of God who takes away the sins of the world, and they become the first two disciples of Jesus. But whereas Andrew goes off to find his brother Peter, the anonymous disciple disappears unnoticed from the story, and reappears only when we find him, twelve chapters later, seated between Jesus and Peter at the Last Supper. Although we are not told this in so many words, the seating arrangements at the Last Supper make it clear that the Beloved Disciple is the host at the meal. Jesus occupies the place of honor on his left, Peter the next most honored position on his right. The Beloved Disciple sits between them. He plays the part of the host at the meal because (this is the only explanation that makes sense) he owns the house where the Supper takes place.

The Beloved Disciple, then, is a resident of Jerusalem. He is not one of those disciples from Galilee who traveled around with Jesus. He is not one of the twelve whom Jesus chose especially to travel with him and to become the leaders of the new Israel. The Beloved Disciple is more like Martha, Mary and Lazarus, a disciple who stays at home and knows Jesus from Jesus' visits to Jerusalem. This is partly why he does not appear in the other Gospels. Ignored in the other Gospels, unobtrusive even in his own, the Beloved Disciple is not, it seems, a major player in Jesus' story. He does very little. In the whole Gospel he speaks only nine words. That's fewer than Mary Magdalene, fewer than Martha or Mary of Bethany, fewer than Philip or Andrew or Thomas, far fewer than Peter. Unobtrusively but significantly he is simply there – close to Jesus at the Last Supper, close to Jesus at the cross, the first male disciple at the empty tomb on Easter morning.

He was not one of those disciples Jesus singled out for leadership, like the Twelve, but he was singled out in another way. He was 'the disciple Jesus loved.' Of course he was not the only disciple Jesus loved. Jesus loved the Bethany family, Martha and Mary and Lazarus, the Gospel tells us in chapter 11. They were Jesus' close friends. Jesus loved all his disciples and loved them to the end, the Gospel tells us at the beginning of the passion narrative. But still the anonymous disciple is 'the disciple Jesus loved.' He alone is called this and he is called nothing else. Though he is with Jesus less of the time than the Galilean disciples are, nevertheless he is the closest to Jesus.

So when Peter and the others have failed Jesus, the Beloved Disciple, like the women disciples, is loyal to the end. He is there in the small group at the foot of the cross with Mary Magdalene, Jesus' aunt Mary and Jesus' mother. And Jesus, seeing his mother and his closest friend – the two people closest to him – there, says to his

mother, 'Here is your son', and to the disciple, 'Here is your mother.'
Jesus' responsibility to care for his mother he hands over to his
friend.

Many commentators want to find some grand theological symbol-
ism in this event, as though it were too trivial for the Gospel to
record if it meant no more than it seems on the surface to mean. But
the surface meaning is not trivial. We should not miss the basic
humanity of Jesus' words. Just as Jesus' agony and desolation are as
human as any, so like anyone facing death Jesus turns to the people
who have meant most to him at the level of human affection: his
mother and his closest friend. His love for all people does not negate
this particular affection for particular people. Jesus acknowledges the
two great forms of human affection – family and friendship – and he
brings them together in entrusting his mother to his friend and his
friend to his mother.

If we insist on seeing more than this in the event, then we must
take that thoroughly human affection of Jesus for his mother and his
friend into the larger meaning, not leave it aside. We could, it has
been suggested, see in this new relationship that Jesus, crucified and
dying, creates between his mother and his friend the beginning of the
Church. It is the first example of the way Jesus' death brings people
together in new relationships given them by Jesus. Just as Jesus'
mother and the Beloved Disciple would not otherwise have been
related, had not Jesus at his death brought them together, and
charged them with being mother and son to each other, so the Church
is the community of people who would not otherwise be related but
whom the crucified Jesus brings together, forging new relationships
through his death for us. But if we do follow this line of thought, then
the thoroughly human reality of what happens at the cross remains
very important. We are not to be concerned with a splendidly abstract
sort of love in which people love humanity but have no real concern
or affection for individuals. The relationships Jesus creates in the
Church are the continuation of his own very human love for his own

mother and the continuation of his own very human affection for his best friend. Moreover, entrusting his mother to his friend means something very practical: the disciple takes her into his own home.

If this is, as it were, the model for relationships in the Church, then the way that Christians should be relating is as though they were Jesus' best friend entrusted with the care of his mother, or as though they were Jesus' mother given his best friend in place of a son. Jesus in his dying did not put human affection to death. He brought it to new life, set it free to run in new channels, at once deepened and extended it. Jesus entrusted us to each other. He charged us all with the responsible care of each other. So the Church is where those who lack family affection should find it. The Church is where those who lack friends should find friends. The Church is where the love of families and friends can be extended to others. The Church is where those who need the support that can come only in close relationships should find it.

Returning to the Beloved Disciple himself, we must now ask: How should we see the cross through the eyes of this disciple? He does not have a dramatic story, like Peter, who is such an impressive character, wants to die for Jesus, fails so pitifully and has to learn through tragic failure what Jesus' death means for him. Undramatically, the Beloved Disciple simply sticks by Jesus. He is the loyal friend who wants simply to be with Jesus to the end. In this he is more like Mary Magdalene, except that she too had a more dramatic history: her deliverance from seven demons. We can imagine, as we have, her desolation on Golgotha, what the darkness of the cross meant particularly for her. What of the Beloved Disciple? The fact is we do not know what the cross meant for him personally and in particular, and we should not try in this case to guess or to imagine. If we did so we would miss this disciple's special significance, which sets him apart from all the other disciples in the story of Jesus' passion and death.

The Beloved Disciple's unobtrusiveness in his own Gospel is not a result of modesty. It is because his role in the story of Jesus is the role

of *witness* to Jesus and his story. The Beloved Disciple is the perceptive witness, the one who is close to Jesus, the one who is close to the
events, the one who therefore understands. His importance is not as
an actor in the story but as a witness to the story and its meaning. He
is there not to make a difference to the events but to observe, to take
it all in, to understand what's going on, to report, to interpret for us,
to take us further into the meaning of it all than anyone else can.

So at the one and only point where he really, obtrusively draws
attention to himself, he speaks of himself and directly to us in this
way: 'He who saw this has testified so that you also may believe. His
testimony is true, and he knows that he tells the truth' (Jn 19:35). He
does not actually want us to know anything else about him personally,
because that would detract from his witness. He does not want us to
get interested in him personally, because as a witness his role is to
show us what he saw. Seeing the cross through his eyes is not seeing
what it meant for him in particular but seeing what it means for all
of us. He is the perceptive witness who points us to what most
deserves our attention. He is the witness who because he was the
closest to Jesus has been able to see furthest into the meaning of the
events. He tells us the story so that we can see both the events as he
saw them and the meaning he came to see in them.

The meaning to which he witnesses, for us as for all readers of the
Gospel, is remarkable. This apparently minor event – the death of
one man, surrounded by a few soldiers and a few friends – has life-
changing, history-changing, world-changing, cosmic meaning. The
witness merely tells us what he saw, and, at first sight, all we see is one
man dying, hanging on just one of the no doubt hundreds of crosses
on which other criminals and outcasts died all over the Roman
Empire on just that one day. It is an ordinary event of no obviously
special significance. The same sort of story could presumably have
been told of many other crucifixion victims, except that no one would
have bothered to tell it. Why be interested in such a man or such an
event? Everything that happens is commonplace. The soldiers cast

lots for the man's tunic. A few relatives and friends, all completely
insignificant people, stand around the cross. The dying man entrusts
his mother to someone. Parched, he cries out for something to drink,
and someone takes pity on him and gives him some sour wine. 'It's
over,' he gasps and dies. The soldiers go around breaking the legs of
the crucified men but find this one already dead. So instead of breaking his legs they thrust a spear in his side.

The story is matter-of-fact observation of a seemingly unremarkable scene. But our witness sees further and lets us see further. He lets
us see the world-changing meaning in these apparently so unremarkable events. He does not do what the other Evangelists do. He does
not surround the cross with cosmic signs of its significance: the darkness at noon, the earthquake, the rending of the veil of the temple.
His rather spare narrative has none of that. It has nothing one might
not observe at another crucifixion. Nothing for a mere onlooker to
remark on. But everything for the perceptive witness to discern. For
the cosmic significance, the world-changing meaning, lies hidden in
the ordinary humanness of this event. The difference from every
other crucifixion, from every other death, is simply this: that on this
cross the God who made the universe dies an utterly human death, no
less human because it is the Creator of all who dies it. This does not
and cannot change its unremarkable humanness but gives it the
remarkable meaning the discerning witness perceives. Seeing the
events through his eyes, sharing both his sight of them and his insight
into them, we see them, ordinary as they are, as the events on which
God's whole purpose for his whole creation hangs.

The point where the witness draws attention to his witness, certi-
fying its reliable truth in the words already quoted above, is not in
fact at Jesus' death but in connection with the events immediately
following Jesus' death. He draws our attention to two aspects of what
he saw. First, Jesus' legs are not broken. Second, from the wound in
Jesus' side both blood and water flow.

Jesus' legs were not broken. As the Scripture said of the Passover

lamb, 'None of its bones shall be broken.' Jesus is therefore seen to be
what John the Baptist had said at the beginning of the Gospel that he
was: the Lamb of God that takes away the sin of the world. He is the
new Passover lamb or rather the Passover lamb for the world. Israel's
Passover lamb had procured Israel's great redemption from slavery
and oppression in Egypt. Jesus is the world's Passover lamb, procuring
the world's redemption, the great exodus of all humanity from
slavery, oppression, sin, evil and death into the freedom of new life
with God. This is the turning-point of history. This shameful death
of an obscure outcast, unnoticed by any Roman historian, is the point
at which God has broken the power of evil in his world and opened
the way to freedom for all.

From the wound in Jesus' side flow both blood and water. What
procured redemption for Israel at the exodus was the sacrifice of the
Passover lamb. Blood had to flow. The blood then is the sacrificial
power of Jesus' death to cleanse us from sin and to deliver us from
evil. But the flow from Jesus' side is also of water – the water of life,
the living water, the life-giving water, the life of God's Spirit that
Jesus had promised he would give. From Jesus' crucified body flow the
blood that takes away the sin of the world and the water that gives life
to the world. The blood purges the past; the water flows into the
future. For all the immeasurable evils of human history and for all
the squalid faults and miserable failures of ordinary human lives,
Jesus' blood flows. And to bring new life to all, new life for wasted and
spoiled and exhausted life, life out of death for all God's dying creation, life springing up eternally and inexhaustibly, the water of life
flows from the side of the crucified Jesus.

These are images, not explanations. And so we may still say, 'After
all, isn't this just an ordinary and insignificant event? Truthful as our
witness's sight may be, can we be so sure of his insight?' To which I
think his only reply is to offer us his testimony: 'The one who saw this
has testified so that you also may believe.' All he can say is: 'Look! See
what I saw. Go on looking until you also see.' And his final Scripture,

his clinching prooftext from the store of prophetic testimonies he cites, is this one from Zechariah: 'They shall look on the one whom they have pierced.' As they look they are moved. The fountain opens. We look at the dead, wounded Jesus, a picture of gruesome cruelty and desolate hopes. We bring our lives into this scene and the crucified Jesus enters our lives. We look until the sight of Jesus, crucified for us, proves the new beginning for us that it is for the world.

For Prayer & Reflection

'Just as I am, without one plea
but that thy blood was shed for me,
and that thou bidst me come to thee,
O Lamb of God, I come.'

Lord Jesus, with the disciple you loved we see your cross,
we see you bow your head and give up your spirit,
we see your side pierced,
we see the blood and the water flow.

Jesus, Lamb of God,
whose blood was shed for us,
you cleanse us from the defilement of sin,
you lift from us the burden of our guilt,
you free us from the tyranny of evil.

Put to death in us all that resists God.
Put behind us all hinders us from living for God.

Jesus, Rock of ages,
from whom the water of life flows,

you satisfy our thirst for true life,
you nourish the shoots of new life in us,
you fill us with your Spirit.

Keep us in the life that in God is alive forever.
Lead us in the life that is ours only as we give it for God and for others.

The Miracle He Didn't Want to Perform

'If you're the Son of God, come down from the cross.' To undo three nails
would have been a mere trifle for a carpenter's son. In Joseph's work-
shop he had worked on wood up to the age of thirty, and there he still
was, stuck between wood and nails. He could tell from the smell and
texture whether this wood was beech, oak or chestnut. Three nails
deeply wedged into the wood's white fibre – how many he had put in
and pulled out! He knew how to do it. It would have been an easy
miracle, scarcely a miracle at all.

The rabble shouted: 'Come down, imposter'; from up above he
could see their mouths opening in blasphemies, their teeth gleaming
in mockery and laughter. He could see the bronzed muscle-work of
their shoulders, and the anxious heads of the soldiers bent over their
dice. He could see his mother like a little black ant who, that evening,
would remain alone on the pavements of the world.

Yes, he'd come down. By now everything had been fulfilled. He
wouldn't take regrets to the Father. For the world to be redeemed the
first tear shed in the garden was enough, the first drop of blood that
spurted under the scourge. It would have been enough to say, 'This is
what I want', without this strange journey into the prison of mankind,
without taking on this flesh which was now one knot of pain. He had
already emptied the cup; his body couldn't suffer any more because it
was no longer a body; the last drop of blood had gone from it. And

dying would be only too easy, it would add nothing to the sacrifice.

It would be a simple and quiet miracle. He would come down as from a ladder. The angels would immediately change the red holes of his wounds into roses and he would reach the ground unharmed. Having reached the ground he would go down the hill. They would go to Lazarus's house in Bethany. That very evening, in the gentle light of the two sisters, Mary would hear him telling wonderful things.

Yes, this was certainly the most necessary miracle if he wanted the world to believe in him. Get down. Nothing else would be needed, and thousands of martyrs would be spared . . .

We would certainly have come down. Our mothers and our common sense would have torn us down with the nails still fixed in our hands and feet. We would have run away, trailing the hill with blood, towards the throne on to which terrified men who realized their mistake would finally raise us.

But he didn't want to work this miracle. The man on the cross knew that if he had done that, with the first contact of his feet with the ground all the other miracles told us in the gospel would have been wiped out: the paralysed man would have lain down again on his pallet, the woman with the flow of blood would have begun to bleed again, the blind people of Jericho would have been plunged back again into darkness, the bodies of the ten lepers would have been racked with old sores, and Lazarus and the others would have disappeared for ever into the tombs he had emptied. Like fish in an immense sea that has unexpectedly dried up, men would have writhed convulsively about in a silent holocaust.

We can't understand. We'll never believe that life is bought with death and this last breath from the breast is worth more than the gold of all the stars weighing on the night. But he who had made life and death and the stars knew it, and his parched mouth answered: 'No.'

Luigi Santucci

Burying the Burden

He ran thus till he came at a place somewhat ascending; and upon that place stood a Cross, and a little below in the bottom a sepulchre. So I saw in my dream, that just as Christian came up with the Cross, his burden loosed from off his shoulders, and fell from off his back; and began to tumble, and so continued to do till it came to the mouth of the sepulchre, where it fell in, and I saw it no more.

Then was Christian glad and lightsome, and said with a merry heart, 'He hath given me rest, by his sorrow, and life, by his death.' Then he stood still a while, to look and wonder; for it was very surprising to him that the sight of the Cross should thus ease him of his burden. He looked therefore, and looked again, even till the springs that were in his head sent the waters down his cheeks. Now as he stood looking and weeping, behold three Shining Ones came to him, and saluted him, with 'Peace be to thee.' So the first said to him, 'Thy sins be forgiven.' The second stripped him of his rags and clothed him with change of raiment. The third also set a mark on his forehead, and gave him a roll with a seal upon it, which he bid him look on as he ran, and that he should give it in the Celestial Gate: so they went their way. Then Christian gave three leaps for joy, and went on singing.

John Bunyan

SOURCES

Chapter 1
Janet Morley, *All Desires Known* (London: SPCK, 1992), p. 100.

Chapter 2
Terry Waite, *Taken on Trust* (London: Hodder & Stoughton, 1993), pp. 1–5.

Chapter 3
Reid Isaac, *Conversations with the Crucified* (New York: Seabury, 1982), pp. 52–4.

Chapter 7
Sheila Cassidy, *Audacity to Believe* (London: Darton, Longman and Todd, new edition, 1992), pp. 107–9.

Chapter 8

Nicholas Wolterstorff, *Lament for a Son* (Grand Rapids, Mich.: Eerdmans, 1987), p. 69.

Luigi Santucci, *Wrestling with Christ*, trans. Bernard Wall (London: Collins, 1972), pp. 201–2.

Chapter 9

G. A. Studdert Kennedy, *The Unutterable Beauty* (London: Hodder & Stoughton, 1941), pp. 44–8.

Chapter 10

Trevor Dennis, *Speaking of God* (London: SPCK, 1992), pp. 83–6.

Chapter 11

Luigi Santucci, *Wrestling with Christ*, trans. Bernard Wall (London: Collins, 1972) pp. 196–8.

John Bunyan, *The Pilgrim's Progress*, ed. J. B. Wharey, rev. ed. Roger Sharrock (Oxford: Clarendon Press, 1960), p. 38.

Lightning Source UK Ltd.
Milton Keynes UK
UKHW02f0649020818
326666UK00010B/401/P

9 780232 523119